12-4-76   25¢

Are you getting all your library offers you? ---

IN

    Books

    Magazines

    Newspapers

    Pamphlets

    Government Documents

    Pictures

    Maps

    Phonograph Records

    Sheet Music

    Story Hours

    Information Service

PL-8

THE LAND AND PEOPLE OF TURKEY

The Land and People of
TURKEY

BY WILLIAM SPENCER

J. B. LIPPINCOTT COMPANY
PHILADELPHIA AND NEW YORK

Portraits of the Nations Series

(93)

11/63

c 16

Contents

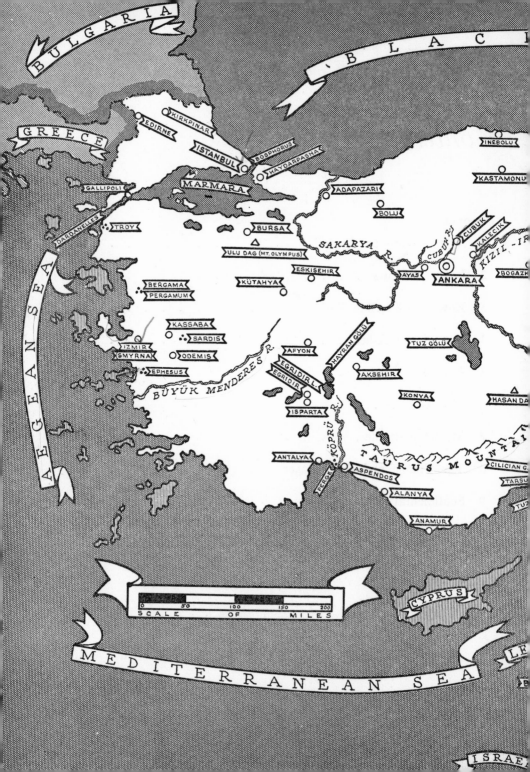

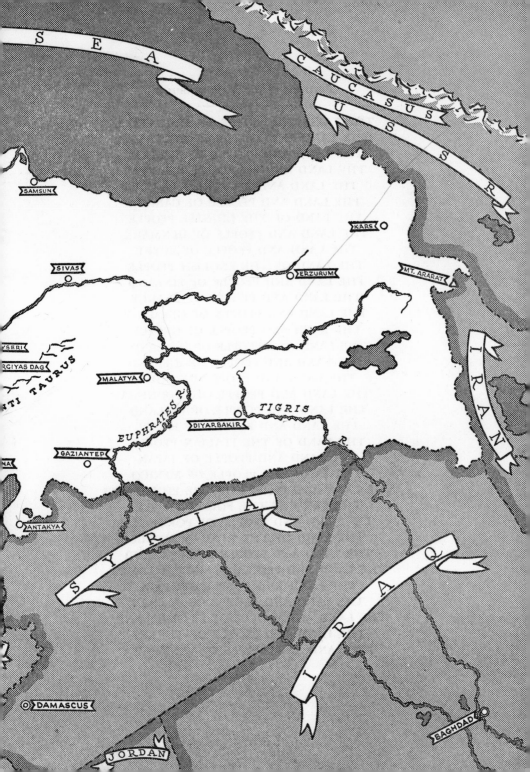

THE LAND AND PEOPLE OF TURKEY

1. Asia Minor—or Anatolia?

THE REPUBLIC OF TURKEY is a long, roughly rectangular peninsula, actually a western projection of Asia. Turkey's three coastlines border three inland seas, the Black (northern), Aegean (western) and Mediterranean (southern). The eastern border meets Soviet Russia and Iran, in a jumbled mass of mountains, the Caucasus and Zagros, with the Anti-Taurus range thrown in for good measure; then it tapers off, moving southward, to meet Iraq in a flat treeless plain. The two great rivers of the ancient Near East, the Tigris and the Euphrates, rise in Turkey and flow south through Syria to irrigate Iraq, the "Land Between the Rivers," finally merging in the Shatt al-Arab, the delta which empties into the Persian Gulf. Turkey's border with Syria is flat and undistinguished, running through farmlands. It hardly seems worth fighting for—but neither does most of the peninsula, and it has been a battleground for thousands of years.

In its northwest corner, between the Black and Aegean Seas, the peninsula is separated from Europe by the narrow channel of the Straits and the Sea of Marmara between the two ends of the channel. Istanbul, Turkey's biggest city and former capital, sits mainly on the European side of the Straits (called the Bosphorus at that point), and Turkish territory continues westward for 166 miles across Thrace to Edirne and the Greek border. Except for this wedge of territory, Turkey is entirely inside Asia; yet the Turks consider themselves Europeans, and look west, not east.

This peninsula, which resembles a buffalo with his head lowered (notice the "eye" of the Marmara Sea glaring at Greece), was called in ancient times Asia Minor. The Greek and Roman writers who named it, such as Herodotus and Thucydides, did so because they believed it was another Asia in miniature. Like Big Asia, Little Asia was a high tableland, with mountains around the rim sloping away to the sea in terraces. There is some truth to this. The mountains of Turkey run more or less parallel to the seas, some distance inland, although occasionally, like Mt. Solyma south of Antalya, they drop straight down within a few hundred feet of the water. They act as shields for the inland plateau, giving it a dry climate with harsh winters and hot summers, in contrast to the mild subtropical climate of the coastal regions. The plateau rises slowly going from west to east, until you reach the highest peak in the country, Mt. Ararat (16,916 feet), where Turkey, Iran, and the Soviet Union meet, and where Noah's Ark is supposedly resting, although the condition of a wooden ship after thousands of years of exposure to Caucasian winters could hardly be good. The Eastern Turkish cities of Kars and Erzurum, traditional gateway for invasions of Asia Minor, are buried under snowdrifts for half the year. Kayseri, in the center of the plateau, has a winter nearly as rigorous. It used to furnish wood for Roman galleys, but is now nearly treeless, and there is nothing to stop the violent winds except mud-brick houses. The area around Kayseri is the dead heart of Asia Minor. Elsewhere the plateau is good wheat country, but a large dead salt lake absorbs what little moisture reaches this area, and life is pretty bleak for the farmers.

Climatically speaking, Asia Minor also resembles Asia in its extremes of temperature. In a journey of perhaps five hundred miles from Istanbul to Ankara and then to Antalya, you change clothes three times as you go from temperate to steppe to subtropical weather conditions.

Politically Asia Minor has achieved its greatest importance as a land bridge to Europe—at least it was the shortest route for invaders or migrating tribes in search of new pastures and new territory. Archaeologists tell us that Central Asia was one of the earliest, if not the earliest, homes of man, and throughout history peoples on the move from Central Asia have crisscrossed Asia Minor. Many of them, of course, settled down and intermarried with the local folk, giving us through this lengthy process the Turks of today.

On at least three occasions in history, the function of the peninsula as a land bridge to Europe brought about events highly significant for civilization. The first of these came when the Persian Emperor Xerxes, having brought his one-hundred-thousand-man army as far on land as they could go, fashioned a bridge of boats across the Dardanelles and went on to be defeated by the Greeks at Marathon. A couple of hundred years later, Alexander the Great reversed the process and brought Greek civilization across Asia Minor, all the way to India. In A.D. 1453 Mehmet II crossed the Bosphorus a third time and captured Constantinople (Istanbul) from the land side, completing the conquest of the Byzantine Greek Empire begun by his ancestors. For that matter, the Crusades, a failure politically but vital in the revival of East-West cultural interchange, all went through the peninsula.

The Turks themselves never speak of their land as Asia Minor. They call it Turkey—but they also speak of "Anatolia," particularly when they are describing the inland plateau. Anatolia (Turkish Anadolu) means land toward the rising sun. It has been settled, fought over, plowed, devastated, replowed, for eons, and for other eons sun and wind worked over this landscape, as if with hammer and chisel and paintbrush. Even today, despite Turkey's increasing industrialization, Anatolia seems timeless. When you drive along one of its dusty roads in a closed automobile insulated from the heat and dust, the country seems merely big and barren. But stop to stretch your legs, and you suddenly realize that you are one small speck, alone in a vast undulating highland. An automobile, of course, is the easy way to see and traverse Anatolia. But see that speck coming nearer? It becomes a man on a donkey—the village schoolteacher going from his home to the village where he teaches. He has ten hours' ride between him and his destination—yet he will know and feel more of Anatolia in that ride than anyone seated behind sealed car windows.

The Anatolian peasant, nurtured in this rugged land, is the backbone of the Turkish nation, as he was of the Ottoman Empire. One Turkish city, Istanbul, has a population of about one and a quarter million; Ankara, the capital, has about five hundred thousand; Izmir two hundred and ninety thousand. Roughly seventy-five per cent of Turkey's population of twenty-six million live in villages, the majority of these on the plateau. In the past, under the Ottomans, the Anatolian peasant was often cruelly exploited, taxed by absentee pasha landlords, conscripted without choice; he grew indifferent to any loyalty but that to his village and the land of his birth. He feels increasing loyalty to his *millet* (nation) now, but his keenest sense is still of his Anatolian homeland.

Turkey is divided into a large number of provinces *(vilayets)* of various shapes and sizes. There are sixty-seven in all. The total area is 296,503 square miles; thus Turkey is slightly larger than Texas. Each vilayet gets its name from its principal town. Even Ankara has a vilayet, and is not separated into an artificial federal district, like Washington or Mexico City. Every vilayet is administered by a *vali*, or governor, who finds time outside of his official duties to welcome all sorts of visitors and get them out of scrapes. I've never known anyone to leave Turkey after a visit for writing, study, or travel purposes, who failed to comment on the hospitality and helpfulness of the valis.

A trip to Turkey is still quite an adventure, particularly as you move from relatively modern Istanbul and other metropolitan areas into remoter Anatolia. You will need, as someone remarked of the equipment an American should carry with him in Asia, the same qualities which distinguished our pioneer ancestors—adaptability to local conditions, a spirit of inquiry, fatalism about time and meeting deadlines, and a stout set of kidneys.

Flying there, your airplane swings over the Aegean Sea, the same one that Homer called "wine-dark" in the *Odyssey*, which incidentally began at ancient Troy, in western Asia Minor. Then the plane swings northeastward, following the silvery line of the Straits, and settles down on the runway of Istanbul's fine modern airport. From there a dual parkway leads to the city, ten miles away. Cruise steamers also follow this route, but give a quite different perspective. You pass rich green wooded slopes, melon fields that go down to the water, and little houses roofed with red tiles. Now and then in a clearing is a *yali*, the former summerhouse of a wealthy Turk. These mansions are built of wood—something you rarely see in the rest of the country—and weathered to a beautiful silver-gray by wind and time and salt air.

Istanbul is not Asia Minor—or Anatolia—however. It has its own special atmosphere. A definite Turkish policy during the Republic was to build up the interior plateau and the relatively backward, provincial cities of Ankara, Kayseri, etc., at the expense of Istanbul and Izmir. The former was synonymous with the Ottoman Government and Turkey's defeat in World War I, the latter with the Greek occupation after the war. A great fire following the Greek evacuation paralyzed Izmir anyway, but Istanbul resisted efforts to downgrade her and has remained a world capital, a magnet for all Turks despite removal of the seat of government and foreign embassies to Ankara. Every Turk who lives in Ankara tries to spend his summer in Istanbul, and great numbers of them do. His apartment in Ankara may be larger and more comfortable, but the Ankara Turk prefers to crowd in with a pack of relatives and friends in Istanbul, because—well, there it is!

In general, Turkey is not a country of regions—a man from the South does not have a southern Turkish accent, or feature dishes like corn pone and yams. There are no special architectural features, nor a sense of developed regional pride, except the one mentioned earlier about Anatolia. This sense of unity has developed since the establishment of the Republic in 1923; the system of the Ottoman Empire of separating minorities and giving them internal freedom weakened their loyalty to the Empire and contributed largely to its failure to grow as a progressive modern state ought to.

But we are getting ahead of our story. The journey from Istanbul airport is an excellent lesson in transporting your mental attitudes from a familiar country to an unfamiliar one. The billboards along the route are a touch of home, but instead of soap, cigarettes, and automobiles, they advertise products of a more practical nature—tires, trucks, ball bearings, and, commonest of all, banks. It seems as if every bank in Turkey has an alert advertising manager; the Yapi ve Kredi Bankasi, the Etibank, the Ziraat Bankasi, and the Iş Bank, to name a few, remind the driver of their excellent interest rates and their sound financial structure. But if the billboards are familiar, the roadside scene is foreign. Men in business suits fill the roadside coffeehouses, drinking small glasses of tea, since coffee is unobtainable, and playing obscure card games. A few naked light bulbs hang on cords over their heads. Invariably an unseen radio blares curious music, a blend of several unknown instruments in a key utterly foreign to the Western idea of harmony; the vocalist singing to this band never seems to change her pitch or lower her voice. You will find a touch of American rhythm, however, in the rock and roll music which has lately become the rage in Turkish coffeehouses.

Entering Istanbul is another experience. West Istanbul's streets are narrow and cobbled; the traffic is appalling as cars and taxis compete with prehistoric streetcars, pedestrians, and men carrying trays of fruit and vegetables on their heads. Then the struggle ends abruptly as you turn into a broad boulevard high over the Bosphorus. For a moment, minarets on the opposite shore and the gleaming modern Istanbul Hilton Hotel are visible. Then, just as abruptly, the boulevard ends, and you turn back into a narrow crowded lane. Istanbul is like that. Unless one owns a villa overlooking the water, one must be content with teasing glimpses, around corners, of the city's aquatic setting.

Istanbul is mostly in Europe, by geography, but much of its personality is non-European. It is first of all an inscrutable city. No one going there for the first time understands it, and the combination of strange food, confusion and inconvenience usually makes one furious, rather than appreciative. You will need a return visit or two before you can believe the guidebooks.

Without further delay, then, suppose we hunt for the best method of transportation to Ankara. We could fly—but do we want to travel thousands of feet in the air *above* Turkey, in a sealed cabin? We could hire a car and drive, but are we ready for the rugged terrain of Anatolia? And we were warned that Turkish drivers are not very dependable. So we decide on the train. There are three a day each way; the *Motorlu,* a diesel which goes by day, or the all-sleeper Orient Express, by night. Ah, this sounds more romantic; besides, we can leave immediately and forget Istanbul for a while. It isn't quite so easy, however; the Istanbul-Ankara train doesn't leave from Istanbul, but from Haydarpasha, across the Bosphorus in Asia. So we hail a *taksi.* Driving downhill from Beyoğlu (the European quarter) much too fast for safety, and banging his hand on the door of his 1946 Ford because horns are forbidden, our taksi driver deposits us on the Galata Bridge, the main artery between two sections of Istanbul which are in Europe. We still have not reached Asia, however; to get there we must take a ferryboat for Haydarpasha, or swim.

Having left the taxi, with our bags, we find ourselves unexpectedly at the mercy of another of Istanbul's essential services, the *hamal,* or porter. I say "mercy" because a horde of these stout fellows fling themselves on our luggage, while we stand helplessly trying to remember the Turkish word for "Stop that." In a very short time one of the hamals has full control of the bags, and we are surprised to see how big he is. He hoists everything on his head, legs, and back, depending on the number of pieces, and off he trots for some unknown destination. There's no use running after him; he knows exactly what he is doing. We won't see him again until, with the help of Allah (and a convenient bystander who speaks English) we have found the proper ferry, walked aboard, and climbed to the upper deck. There he is, squatting on our bags. Not a thing is missing; he even has our tickets. We look him over: about twenty, stocky, strong in shoulders and arms, smooth skin, between white and tan in color, deep brown eyes, slick black hair, pomaded, a narrow mustache giving him a sinister look. He wears a patched jacket and trousers, and tennis shoes. Imagine how easy it would be for this hamal to disappear into the narrow crowded streets with all our bags, and sell them for half a year's wages! Yet nothing is missing; nothing is *ever* missing. It is the first of many contradictions in the Turkish character we will find.

Swinging from side to side with the strong current, the ferry labors toward the opposite shore. We worry about missing our train while our Turkish fellow-passengers sit stolidly, certain that they will arrive somewhere, preferably but not necessarily the rail terminus. And after all it is a beautiful evening. Behind are the city's seven hills and its red tile roofs, its wooden houses. The buildings are dwarfed by the Galata Fire Tower, where a twenty-four hour watch is kept in this most combustible of all cities.

Across the Golden Horn some of the wonders of Istanbul's skyline emerge—Santa Sophia, the Palaces, the Blue Mosque of Sultan Ahmed. In the center of the Bosphorus is the erroneously-named Leander's Tower, a lonely shaft which commemorates the legend of Leander and Hero. Hero was a priestess who lived in *another* tower at the other end of the Straits, then called the Hellespont. Leander, who loved her, lived on the opposite shore, and every night for months used to swim across the narrow Hellespont to see his sweetheart. His luck finally ran out and he was drowned in rough water.

This Bosphorus is Istanbul's trademark; the city would be nothing without it. It is full of activity in the early evening, as boys dive from pilings, and fish with rods cut from straight poplar trees. Along the shore old men puff their *narghiles* (water pipes) at café tables under the ancient plane trees; families watch this bustle from the upper balconies of their silvered wooden houses. The white ferryboats send up little flares of spray as they cross each other's paths. There is Dolma Bahçe, one of the great palaces of the sultans, looking exactly like Versailles on the waterfront. Flocks of shearwaters, a strange northern bird, skim low over the water, uttering their haunting lonely call as if they were searching for some lost soul. We are more kindly disposed toward Istanbul as we board our train and creak away toward inland Anatolia. Soon the city is far behind, and the rock of the wheels lulls us to sleep and dreams of the rich past of this peninsula which is now Turkey.

2. Long Shadows

WE DON'T KNOW VERY MUCH about the first citizens of Anatolia, but very likely the peninsula was inhabited from an extremely early time, and has been civilized for probably as long as any other stretch of the globe. The Bible dates mankind from Adam, and a common theory holds the original Garden of Eden to be somewhere between the Tigris and Euphrates rivers in what is now Iraq. Of course Adam and Eve spent but a short period of their lives in the Garden; most of their years were spent wandering. There is a legend in Anatolia which may cast some light on the beginnings of life there. According to the legend, Adam, old and tired and ready to give up life, made a last request of the angel sent to bring him to God. "Before I go," he said, "let me look once upon my birthplace. I have been away for so long that I have forgotten where it is." The angel agreed, and off they went. They searched everywhere, in all the known and unknown lands, and nothing he saw reminded Adam of his birthplace. Finally Adam gave up, and they started back for the Garden of Eden. On the way they passed over eastern Anatolia; Adam looked down at men threshing with wooden flails, carts with solid wooden wheels, women bent double in the dusty fields, mud-brick houses under a fierce sun. "That is my birthplace!" he declared.

It may be more than coincidence that the Turkish word for *man* is *adam*. The anthropologist Carleton Coon says that Western man's original home was somewhere along the northern shore of the Caspian

Sea. This would seem to indicate that even before people began to keep records, nomadic tribes, urged on by some dim instinct that better grazing lands lay to the west, were moving across the land bridge of Asia Minor. Always west, never east. In fact a common theme in classical Turkish poetry pictured the Turks as an army of horsemen, disciplined and silent, riding out of the dawn toward the sunset.

One of the most fascinating qualities of Anatolia is that even today, after four thousand years of recorded history and thousands more of unrecorded, this rugged land is as timeless as ever. A few minutes' drive out of Ankara, and civilization has disappeared. All around you is an empty landscape. The dominant color is brown, but glints of different colors occasionally flash in the sun from minerals in some barren rock. The dominant mood is silence. I remember on my first trip across Anatolia, waking up one morning early. The train had stopped at some apparently deserted way station; the sun was already climbing the horizon. I listened for the customary sounds of a train halt—water tanks, coal being poured into coal cars, shouts of village people running to wave at the passengers, machinery grinding. But there was not a sound. It was almost impossible to realize, in our modern noisy civilized world, that one could be in a place where there was only silence. But that is Anatolia.

Even today there is a thrill over every ridge in this land—a new village, some ruins, an extinct volcano. Imagine how the migrating tribesmen must have felt four thousand years ago, crossing without any idea of what lay ahead. No wonder many of them settled wherever they could find water, protection, and pasturage. This is surely how Anatolia was settled, in little pockets unaware of each other until travelers came along to tell them about the outside world.

There are no navigable rivers in Anatolia, and the more energetic of the nomads pushed on until they reached the seas, where they turned into seafarers, traders and middlemen (and incidentally, colonists). These were the Minoans of Crete, the Phoenicians, the Achaeans and Greeks. Those who stayed in Anatolia remained sheepherders and goatherders, and of necessity farmers. The slow rhythm of rural life in Anatolia established then, though often submerged by foreign invasion, remains much the same; the unmortared mud-brick houses of the villages crumble slowly under the baking sun, or wash away in the spring rains, and are as slowly rebuilt. Today's subtle difference is, however, noticeable; for only the second time in their history the durable peasant stock of Anatolia are a favored part of a strong and unified nation.

A number of the invading civilizations which passed over the peninsula and were grafted onto its basic stock, used better building materials than mud brick. From a construction standpoint the grandest of these civilizations was the property of a people absolutely lost to the world less than a hundred years ago, who founded a great empire in central Anatolia twenty-five centuries before the Christian era. In that far-off time they built cities, dug wells, laid sewers, and invented several new devices for war. Yet except for a string of lucky coincidences we still would know next to nothing about them.

This first great people of Anatolia were the Hittites. The Bible refers to them in a few places as one of a number of lesser tribes in Syria-Palestine. An important German encyclopedia of 1871 gives them seven lines of information, all wrong. Yet once in the Old Testament (II Kings 7:6) a statement occurs which should have set people thinking. The statement reads: "and they [the Syrian warriors] said one to another, Lo, the King of Israel hath hired against us the kings of the Hittites, and the kings of the Egyptians, to come upon us." To mention the Hittites in the same breath as Egypt, the superpower of that day, should have aroused some curiosity—or should it? In 1834 an adventurous Frenchman named Charles Texier was wandering about Anatolia, trying to find a vanished Gallic city called Tavium, of no particular importance except that he was an archaeologist, hence all lost cities were important. Near the village of Boğazköy, east of modern Ankara, Texier got a tip from some villagers about stone carvings above their village on a plateau. He struggled up a rough cart track on the face of the ridge, and emerged in the middle of a fantastic collection of architecture. Huge blocks of granite were lying or standing everywhere on the mile-long plateau. Many were carved in the shapes of crude but recognizable lions, winged monsters, and men. In a cleft nearby was a bas-relief of a procession of people led by a priest, obviously going to a temple to worship. The figures were racially unknown to Texier—short stocky bodies, broad flat foreheads, huge hooked noses. As he traced the outlines of tremendous fortifications, and looked at the savage landscape around the ruined city, it seemed to the archaeologist that only some wealthy and powerful nation could have built such a city. Yet he knew of no such civilization existing in the past in Anatolia.

We now know that Texier had discovered, or rediscovered, the capital city of the Hittites, Hattusas, and that the Hittites were a world power between 2000 and 1100 B.C., equal at times to Egypt. Discoveries of other Hittite centers nearby, called after their modern names Alacahöyük and Yazilikaya followed, and then Hittite inscriptions, tablets, and ruins began turning up all over Turkey and Syria and even Iraq. It became obvious that the Hittites were to be mentioned in the same sentence with Egypt, and that the Bible was right. We won't go into the archaeological hunches that proved to be correct—you can read the whole story in C. W. Ceram's fascinating book *The Secret of the Hittites*. The key break, of course, came not in 1834, but in 1190 B.C., when foreign invaders burned Hattusas. The conflagration, which must have lasted for days, ironically preserved what was left of the city in its own ashes and dust, until it was rediscovered thirty centuries later.

We really ought to travel to Hattusas to introduce ourselves to Anatolian history and its strange fusion of past and present. It is 120 miles north-northeast of Ankara. Climbing on stabilized but winding and dangerous roads, we cross shale-strewn ridges in a setting as barren as the moon. Then abruptly, in a magic Anatolian change of scenery, we enter a wide valley and go along parallel to a river the color of dried blood. This is the Kizil Irmak, the Red River of the Turks, and the Halys River of classical antiquity. It flows in the shape of a sickle through north-central Anatolia to the Black Sea, and it formed the border of the Hittite Empire. When the Hittites were strong, they called the people west of the river barbarians, and when they were conquered, the Phrygians west of the river called the easterners barbarians. Thus the Halys was the first Iron Curtain.

At the village of Boğazköy, literally Village of the Narrow Gorge, we ask directions and find ourselves a guide, less for the information he can give us on the site—he speaks no English—but because his presence deters the various urchins and hangers-on who would otherwise accompany us. Something about the grandeur of this setting makes you want to be *alone*. We pound up a rutted jeep road nearly as rough as it was in Texier's day, but wider. The *bekçi* (watchman) says that one must be careful during the rains because it's quite possible to climb the ridge on a dry morning and find the road washed out in the afternoon.

We sign the guestbook at a small hut that serves as a gatehouse. There are no pamphlets, no souvenirs, no Coca-Cola; in fact, the only way to make a tourist overnight trip here is to camp among the ruins. The bekçi shows us around. There is the broad excavation of the national Hittite archives, where the first collection of clay tablets was dug up. We can see the extent and heat of the fire by noting how crumbled and wedged together are the remaining bricks of the building which contained these archives. Nearby is a temple outline and the long lines of an outer wall of fitted granite blocks. It is almost impossible to believe that these blocks were formed with hand tools, iron-tipped chisels and hammers. Another square stone block attracts our attention; one side has been hollowed and shaped into a shallow basin. A bathtub? A washbasin? A place for offerings? Nobody knows; it is just one of the many unsolved mysteries of this intelligent and practical people.

There is nothing mysterious, however, about the Lion Gate. Still standing are two parallel columns of huge blocks, twenty feet high and fitted together as smoothly without mortar as any modern concrete building; one is carved into the mane and head of a perfectly normal, recognizable lion (its mate was carried off to the Hittite Museum in Ankara). The lion, says the bekçi, was a Hittite symbol, although it's a moot point whether or not there ever were lions in Anatolia. The Turkish word for lion is *arslan,* and it used to be applied freely as an epithet to particularly brave Turkish warriors.

One other example of Hittite ingenuity is worth mentioning. Hattusas was protected on three sides by cliffs, but the fourth side faced on broken country, although partially blocked by a low ridge. The Hittites built a wall on the ridge, then tunneled *under* it, so that whenever the city was under siege they could sneak out at night for surprise attacks. The tunnel was fitted with the same big blocks. After three thousand years it is still in good repair, and we find we can walk through standing up!

It is time to leave the Hittites, but we ought to give them a moment of respectful silence, as we watch the sun setting behind the blood-red Halys in the distance. Hittite military men developed the two-man chariot with open-spoked wheels into the finest offensive weapon of its time. Hittite kings with such wonderful names as Suppiluliumas and Asitawandas built a federated empire not only by conquest but by treaty and royal marriages; in fact a Hittite princess became the wife of one of Egypt's great Pharaohs. Such Hittite documents as the great treaty between them and Rameses of Egypt have not been bettered by twentieth-century diplomats. It is a little sad to reflect that this great civilization was put to the torch by crude barbarians, and that now sheep graze and farmers plant wheat in the streets of Hattusas.

The nations who came to power in Anatolia after the Hittites kept piling up layers of civilization. An easy way to visualize this is to look at the northwest corner of the peninsula, near the Dardanelles Straits, at a mound called Hisarlik. This is the site of Troy, the city of the *Iliad* and *Odyssey,* of Homer's story—on this mound Greek Achilles, Nestor and Ulysses, fought Priam and Paris and Hector. But if you dug into the mound, you would find nine separate cities, each on top of the

previous one; and the question is, Which Troy? Actually the archaeologist Schliemann, who first identified the mound, picked the wrong city.
The important thing is not, "Which Troy?" but that three thousand
years ago there was already a permanent culture in Asia Minor.

Troy was captured not long after the burning of the Hittite capital,
and this capture opened the way for widening Greek colonization of
western Asia Minor. An infinite variety of people has settled there in
the intervening generations, intermarried, conquered and were conquered. And there developed from this a basic Anatolian character. It
was characterized by several qualities—an attachment to the land, a
spirit of independence, a trading instinct, a love of the sea and the high
mountains. The rugged inland climate of Anatolia bred a hardy, vigorous people, predominantly Turkish; the gentler seacoast produced a
different breed. What held them together was the bond of Anatolia.

The great period in Anatolia-Asia Minor's commercial expansion
came between the fall of Troy and the decline of the Roman Empire.
The area has many natural resources—tin, chrome, copper, olives, fruit
in abundance, wheat. Until they were cut over, trees were also plenti-
ful; the Roman navy got the wood for its galleys from Asia Minor,
particularly from around modern Ankara, a region devoid of forest
today except where the Republican Government has begun reforestation
programs. Best of all, for the Greeks and Romans at least, was the
presence of great deposits of the very finest marble in the ancient
world. Marble from Ionia and Caria near the Aegean Sea was used in
the building of such wonders of that time as the Mausoleum at Halicarnassus and the Temple of Diana at Ephesus.

Thus Asia Minor developed an early preference for trade over
adventuring. The great trade highways from China, India and Persia,
the spice and silk routes, crisscrossed the peninsula. Around natural
harbors, now unfortunately clogged with silt, wealthy commercial cities
grew up. We will see how rich these were when we go to visit them.

As noted, most of the Greek speaking peoples settled in the western
part of Asia Minor. Between them and the remains of the Hittite Em-

pire were two peoples we ought to know something about: the Phrygians and the Lydians. The Phrygian kingdom left us two personalities the modern Turks are very proud of, just as they like to trace their descent from the Hittites in order to claim a continuous Turkish history for Anatolia. The first of these personalities was Gordius, who was anything but a king at the beginning of his career. In fact, he was an ordinary Anatolian farmer. It so happened that his people, the Phrygians, had decided to elect themselves a king, and as no suitable candidate had appeared they asked the local oracle to name one, or at least tell them how they might find one. The oracle, in the customary inscrutable fashion of oracles, predicted that the first person to pass by his shrine riding in a cart would be the proper king. The Phrygian elders rushed out to the road, and there was poor Gordius in his cart, driving his oxen to market. So he was made king and oddly enough, considering the circumstances of his selection, he was a pretty good king. He expanded Phrygia into a stable and respectable kingdom, and built a capital city, named Gordium, naturally, alongside the oracle which had given him his start in life.

Gordius was very proud of his ox cart, because the knot tying the pole of the cart to the axletree was an especially intricate one. It was made from the bark of the cornel tree, which has very tough wood. He used to challenge people to untie it, and no one could. The obliging oracle then predicted that the first person to untie the knot would rule over all Asia. Long after Gordius had died, the knot stood in Gordium hurling a perpetual challenge at all knot-untiers. At last Alexander the Great came there on his way to fight the Persians, and simply cut the knot in two with a slice of his sword. Then he went on to conquer Asia. So "cutting the Gordian knot" is an Anatolian way to solve your difficulties.

One of Gordius's successors was named Midas—actually all Phrygian rulers were either Midas or Gordius—but this Midas had a rather peculiar gift. He was able to turn everything he touched into gold, even his daughter, as he discovered one evening to his eternal regret. This may have proved the Phrygians were a very imaginative race, but again a legend of ancient Anatolia, that of the "golden touch" has passed into our own civilization. When we say a person has this golden touch, we mean he is very lucky indeed.

Another rich man who belonged to this region and left us a legacy was Croesus. He was king of the Lydians, a people who got their start by virtue of holding territory along the east-west caravan road and charging tolls to passing camel caravans. In addition to this revenue, a Lydian king like Croesus had only to scoop up a handful of sand from the bed of the Pactolus River, flowing through Sardis, his capital, to find a month's wages in loose gold. However, while King Midas may have starved to death with his golden touch, Croesus made a different mistake. Before leading his army against the upstart Persians who had invaded Lydia, he asked *his* oracle for the usual advice. The oracle told him that before sunset a great empire would be destroyed. "Good!" said Croesus, and went happily off to war. Before sunset a great empire *was* destroyed, but it proved to be his own.

The Lydians also gave the world two other inventions, the idea (as well as the visible figure) of a tyrant, and money. Since they were the middlemen in trade between East and West, they found they needed some sort of official exchange to inspire confidence in those they dealt with. They began putting a government stamp—a lion or a fox—on the metal discs they used to make purchases or trades. If all our problems are traceable to too much or too little money, blame the Lydians.

After the defeat of Croesus the Persians became rulers of Asia Minor, but they were far away and operated through provincial governors, leaving commercial development operations largely untouched. The irregular wars between Athenians and Spartans and Persians passed western Anatolia by, for the most part. In 449 B.C., an unusual treaty was concluded which limited the Persian king and his forces to the distance of a day's journey on horseback from the sea; also, the king was forbidden to send his ships into the Aegean harbors and islands. In the third century B.C. Alexander the Great, after he had hacked through the Gordian knot, became the next foreign invader to control the peninsula. After Alexander died at the age of twenty-three, Asia Minor was split up among quarreling Macedonian generals. The Ionian cities, their trade reduced by political insecurity, began to look longingly westward, toward the new city-state of Rome.

The kingdom of Pergamum, in western Asia Minor, was not the first small state in the peninsula to become part of the expanding Roman power, but its method is interesting, and illustrates again how much we owe Anatolia and how rich has been her political history. The kings of Pergamum allied themselves with Rome from time to time in the second century B.C. and profitably expanded their territory as Rome expanded. Eventually they grew tired of the responsibilities of running a kingdom, and the last king, Attalus III, bequeathed Pergamum to Rome by a will on his deathbed.

The Romans themselves, once they had united Anatolia, placed a Pax Romana on the peninsula; they gave it law, order, public security, good roads, and efficient administration. Theirs was certainly the best foreign conquest, from the viewpoint of the native Anatolians. Along Turkey's southern coast are the well-preserved ruins of many great cities, with theaters and aqueducts and forts along a chain of hills that made up a system of defense and signals—all left from the Roman period. In fact, this southern road and a large number of other roads are laid on the base of the old Roman military highways.

While it was under Roman occupation, Asia Minor figured largely in the religious life of the Empire—not the pagan religious life, but the Christian. Tarsus, in southern Turkey, was the home of Saul, who changed miraculously from an active persecutor of early Christians to Christianity's greatest spokesman and advocate. St. Paul preached his first sermon after his conversion in Perge, near Antalya in the south and a city previously dedicated to pagan gods. There are letters in the Bible from Paul to the Galatians—people of Gallic descent who lived around Ankara—and the people of Ephesus. When Paul sailed to Ephesus it was the richest city in Ionia—furthermore, it was a city that worshipped the Greek goddess Diana, and had built her a temple considered to be one of the Seven Wonders of the World. Paul's preaching and letter writing in Ephesus were so successful that the supporters of Diana began to worry. Those who worried most were the silversmiths, who got their income from the sale of little silver models of the temple. When Paul tried to give one of his sermons, they started a riot, hooted him down, and paraded through the streets shouting, "Great is Diana of the Ephesians!" Needless to say, the pagan silversmiths were "reconstructed" by certain Roman officials and soldiery, and Ephesus became, in time, a stronghold of Christianity.

So much so, in fact, that a very curious legend developed, and became "fact." Before His crucifixion, Jesus had left His mother in the care of St. John. The legend is that the Virgin Mary came to Ephesus, lived there for many years in a little house above the city, and died there. The modern Turks, who have no particular feelings in the matter, have a house on the mountain which they will show to visitors as the Panaya Kapulu, Our Lady of the Gate, where Mary lived. Her grave, has yet to be found, but the Catholic Church recognizes the place as the Shrine of Mary.

Roman rule in Asia Minor lasted for roughly five hundred years. However, at the end of the fourth century A.D. the Empire divided into two halves. East Rome, with its capital at Constantinople, renamed and rebuilt by Emperor Constantine over the minor Greek city of Byzantium, became custodian of Asia Minor. After West Rome ended politically in A.D. 476, East Rome carried on for a thousand years as the Byzantine Empire.

The Byzantine emperors realized early the importance of Anatolia to the stability of their empire, and accorded it a favored status; its decline was caused primarily by the loss of this territory to the Selcuk Turks, after the defeat at Manzikert (Malazgirt) in 1071. It is proof of Mustafa Kemal's genius that in rallying Turkey after the disastrous defeat of 1918, he started to build with Anatolia.

Favoritism toward Anatolians was managed in various ways. The administrators of its provinces *(themes)* were better paid and more carefully selected than those in the Balkan possessions. Military leaders of skill were given hereditary fiefs of land. And political and military advancement were easier and quicker if one was an Anatolian. It just happened to work out that way. However, Anatolia was not only valuable but vital. The eastern themes were front lines of defense on the borders of Persia and later against the Arabs of the Islamic Caliphate. The best soldiers and sailors for the imperial forces were recruited from the sturdy peasantry. On the borders lived the *akritai,* feudal knights who held fiefs there and fought the infidel for the glory of God and the Emperor and the sheer pleasure of combat.

Great landed estates grew up in Anatolian territory during the Byzantine period, and the leading families of the Byzantine aristocracy were Anatolians. They had a custom of sending at least one member to serve the emperor at Constantinople. Often a feudal baron would appear with a whole regiment of his retainers for army service, notably in time of danger. Considering that the barons were practically independent in their own lands, this devotion to a distant crown is quite surprising. But Christianity was deep and strong in Anatolia, and the emperor, as temporal representative of Christ, merited and could command devotion. Some of these important families not only contributed support and troops, but emperors as well, notably the Phocas family, the Comneni (four emperors), the Macedonian dynasty, (actually Armenian) (A.D. 867-1025), who held control during Byzantium's best years, and others.

The snobbishness and pride of the Anatolian barons, however, was an eventual source of weakness in the empire. When non-Anatolian emperors ruled, the barons frequently ignored calls for aid, and the Fourth Crusade, in which crusaders led by greedy Venetians sacked Constantinople instead of going to Jerusalem, succeeded due to this haughtiness.

Life in Asia Minor under the Byzantines was placid, except for occasional Arab and Persian raids, and emphasized trade and agriculture.

Greek was the language, and Greek Orthodox Christianity the religion. The farmers of the eighth century were fortunate in that their land was fertile and well watered. An inventory of the possessions of a middle-class landowner (not a baron) which has come down to us lists fifty farms, with six-hundred head of cattle, one-hundred oxen, eight-hundred horses, eighty draft horses and mules, and twelve thousand sheep. He could seat thirty-six at the ivory dining table in his manor-house.

Life was harder for the poorer farmers, but still bearable. The farmer and his wife worked their own land, bought their animals on credit, and lived in a house full of relatives. But there were always village pleasures, the weddings, harvests, festivals, and the funerals, too. Constantinople was near enough for travelers enjoying the sacred law of Anatolian hospitality to thrill the dinner-table audience with tales of the great city, "like a young girl, bedecked with gold and precious stones." Most families had a son in the army, and when he came home he had more stories to tell, of barbarian Varangians and Bulgars, and pine forests in the far north.

The eternal threat of invasion, although far away for most of this period, was a heady stimulant for adventurous young men. First it was the Persians; but in the seventh century the Emperor Heraclius lifted the siege of Constantinople and drove them all the way back to Persia. The Arabs posed a longer and more serious threat. The Byzantine Emperor, vicar of Christ and self-appointed lord of all eastern Christians, was their most dangerous enemy as they expanded their empire. Twice they besieged Constantinople, the first time for four years. On the second occasion Anatolia's value to the Empire was proved almost miraculously when the imperial general, Leo the Isaurian (named because he was originally a peasant conscript from the district of Isauria in the southern mountains) marched overland with an army and took the Arab forces by surprise, routing them. A few days later Leo became Emperor Leo V.

The Arabs nibbled away at Anatolia, but never detached much of it. But it made life on the frontiers exciting, both for the akritai and their equally proud, rash, chivalrous Arab opposite numbers, the desert chieftains. The most famous of the akritai, Digenis, had a castle on the Euphrates as elegant as any in the Baghdad of this Arabian Nights time, and Digenis himself, who was probably in fact a treacherous robber, is still celebrated in Anatolia as a kind of Robin Hood, fighting a righteous battle against an unscrupulous Arab sheriff of Nottingham.

The Byzantine era in Anatolian history was certainly brave and colorful, but it could not last. In far-off Central Asia wars and population pressure, as the stronger nomadic tribes appropriated water and grazing lands, drove the weaker nomads westward, along the old migratory road. These nomads drifted into north Persia, where they came in contact with Moslem missionaries. The simple faith and limited requirements of the new religion appealed to them, and they were converted in numbers. Many then formed into bands of *Ghazis* (defenders of the Faith), although most of them simply traveled in tribal groups, looking for pasturage. Few in number but disciplined natural soldiers, stubborn and persistent, and native administrators, they succeeded where the more individualistic Arabs had failed. The consequences of this for Anatolia were immense, and in time largely unfortunate.

3. Enter the Terrible Turk

*L*ONG AGO, according to the epic literature of Central Asia, an army of horsemen appeared on the steppes, riding west toward the setting sun. Behind them trailed their women and children, their carts, their black felt tents. They were led by a gray wolf. This, say the epics, was the historical beginning of the Turkish people.

No one knows exactly how or why the gray wolf became the symbol of the Turks. Some of the old storytellers of Samarkand used to pass along a tale that a Central Asian princess was captured by a band of robbers, then rescued by a gigantic wolf. She married the wolf out of gratitude, and their children became the Turks, gifted beyond other peoples by their combination of human and wolf characteristics. In another legend a she-wolf found an abandoned baby boy and nursed him back to health; the boy grew up in the wolf pack. According to legend, Rome was founded by Romulus and Remus, twin boys suckled by a she-wolf, and although the Turks scorned the Byzantines, they liked to compare themselves to the old Romans. The early Turks were in fact rather like the Romans, disciplined soldiers, administrators, poor traders, and extremely successful empire-builders.

Perhaps there never was such a gray wolf, but the Turkish horsemen who rode out of the steppes to harry Byzantium's frontiers carried a banner with a wolf's head on it. Their tactics, too, seemed to be those of the wolf-pack sneak attacks, sham retreats, swift encirclements by small groups of hard-riding archers. The bugles and kettledrums and whistles would blast the air, the wolf's head standard would be lowered, and the Turks would charge, shouting weird cries and riding around the Byzantines to shoot arrows from all angles. The Crusaders had equally unpleasant experiences. Though protected by armor, after twenty minutes or so of having Turkish archers ride around them shooting arrows, the Crusader knights would begin to look like pincushions, or possibly porcupines. Equally frustrating to Crusader and Byzantine forces was the Turkish habit of attacking quickly and retreating just as quickly; but the Turks were merely applying the tactics they had learned in the endless no-quarter struggle between the nomad tribes of Central Asia.

The origin of the name "Turk" is also shrouded in mystery. According to one theory the word meant helmet, and was given to these raiders because of the battle caps they wore, and their conical black felt tents. These are called *yurts*, and the nomads of High Asia still use them. The Turks were originally a Ural-Altaic people, living in scattered clans in Central Asia; they shared in the great nomad migrations which produced such leaders as Genghis Khan. They first entered the pages of history in the tenth and eleventh centuries A.D. In the seventh century an Arabian prophet named Mohammed had founded a new religion, Islam, and his successors, acting in his name as caliphs, or "Regents of God," had founded an empire stretching from Spain to the borders of China. This empire split up very quickly, but Moslem missionaries went right on converting people to the new religion. Among others they converted was a Central Asian tribal leader named Selcuk, who had settled with his clan near Bokhara in what is now Soviet Russian territory. In Central Asia a clan takes its name from its elected leader, and consists of a group of families, usually related. Selcuk's clan were originally animists; they worshipped the spirits of trees and mountains, as the American Indians did. But these spirits were not too satisfactory, and had not helped them keep their lands and grazing pastures from their enemies. The Selcuk clan was ready for conversion, and Islam got there first. These Turks, or rather Turkomans, (meaning wanderers) were also attracted by the simple requirements of the new faith. All they had to do was to accept One God (Allah) in place of their spirits, learn the precepts of the Koran, the Moslem Bible, pray regularly, and fight the infidel. They liked the last one best, and were so good at it that the caliphs began hiring them for their personal body-guards and elite troops.

Selcuk's sons and grandsons soon began to style themselves Selcuk Turks. Tughrul Beg, their first strong leader, drove the Persians from Baghdad, capital of the Caliphate, and for his pains received the title of Sultan. His son, a chap with the romantic name of Alp Arslan (Lion-Hero) did even better. He brought the Turks into Anatolia to stay. In the year 1071 Alp Arslan and a band of horse-archers met a gigantic Byzantine Army led by Emperor Romanus Diogenes himself near Manzikert (Malazgirt) in eastern Anatolia. The Byzantines were far from home, tired of marching, their ranks full of unpaid mercenaries, and led by a philosopher. They were routed and lost their emperor in the process. From thenceforth the Turks controlled the destinies of the peasant farmers and shepherds of the peninsula.

The Selcuks were not the ones who made "Turk" a bad word used to frighten Balkan children, however. They actually did a great deal for Anatolia. Under their best sultans, their sultanate of Rum (Rome) was well-governed and tolerably secure. Oriental poets and philoso-phers like Mevlana, founder of the Whirling Dervishes, flocked to Sultan Alaeddin Kaikobad's court at Konya in the thirteenth century, while the Mongols were overrunning Europe and Asia. The Selcuks rebuilt the Roman road system and added good highway accommoda-tions (for the time) in their *hans* (inns), plus a chain of watchtowers for security and warning of raids.

At heart the Selcuks remained traveling men, without the capac-ity to govern large territories which distinguishes the real from the ephemeral in great powers. Their cousins the Karamanian Turks, who overran southern Turkey, shared this weakness. Also a factor in the decline of the early Turkish powers was the Crusades. Anatolia is a land bridge from north to south as well as from east to west, and the Crusaders, fired up to regain Jerusalem from the Moslems, marched and rode across it. After beating Sultan Kiliç Arslan (Lion-sword) in the famous battle of Dorylaeum, near the modern Eskişehir and recapturing several cities for the Byzantines, the weary First Crusade forces stopped at Konya and stayed several months, reportedly entranced by the wonderful climate and the Konya pears, famous ever since.

The Turks who put an end to Anatolian insecurity, more or less, for five centuries were the Ottomans. Originally a small clan and a dependency of the Selcuks, the Ottomans expanded rapidly from a corner of the peninsula, profiting by the weakness of their neighbors and their strategic location and opportunism. We call them Turks, but they called themselves Osmanlis, "sons of Osman." *Turk* meant a rude and barbarous and bad-mannered fellow to them.

These Ottomans first entered Anatolia as a band of four-hundred families led by one Ertoghrul, "the Right-Hearted." In their wanderings in search of pasturage Ertoghrul and his men stumbled into a battle. One side was getting the worst of things. The question before them, was, which side should they help? Ertoghrul's men prudently suggested they help the stronger, but Ertoghrul convinced them the manly part was to aid the weaker. So they jumped into the fight, and soon the Tartars, who had been ahead, were running for their lives. The weaker side proved to be Selcuks, led (if we can believe the convenient tradition) by the sultan himself. The sultan was naturally grateful, and gave Ertoghrul a fief of land southwest of Constantinople, on his border with the Byzantines. A star was born.

Ertoghrul has always been given short shrift in the history books. His son Osman, luckier at least in his name, left this as a heritage to his people. Ertoghrul was also a pagan, but Osman turned Moslem, supposedly after reading a copy of the Koran all the way through, *standing up,* one night at the house of a pious Moslem friend. Anyway Islam gave the Ottomans what they were lacking—a world religion and a ready-made political organization. Admittedly the organization was run-down and needed help, but it gave the Ottomans the right and the way to world conquest. It was the final missing piece in the mosaic of Ottoman fortunes, and enabled an obscure tribe to become world leaders.

Osman and the eight sultans who followed him were brilliant leaders and excellent administrators, and their empire expanded steadily till at its greatest extent, under Sulayman the Magnificent (1520-1566), it stretched from the eastern border of Morocco to the edge of Persia, and from the Caucasus to Arabia's southern spice coasts. The early sultans also governed well. Once they had defeated a Christian country, like Hungary, they placed it under an Ottoman governor but left internal administration in the hands of the local population. The energy and ability of the first eight descendants of Osman was matched only by the degeneracy and ineffectuality of the rest, who let the empire dribble away in three hundred and fifty years.

Two sultans require special mention. The first, Mehmet II, is still a Turkish hero although Turkey has turned its back on the Ottomans. He is always called Mehmet *Fatih* (Conqueror) because he captured Constantinople. This happened on May 29, 1453, but as any student of Greek-Turkish relations will testify, it is a date still very much alive in Greek hearts, and all road signs in Greece point to Constantinople, although Mehmet changed the name to Istanbul. In fact the capture of the city was a blessing in many ways, although none of the western powers of that age lifted a finger to help the last emperor, Constantine XII. The city had degenerated and become a veritable pool of corruption; Mehmet Fatih and his engineers cleaned it up, and his architects beautified the city's skyline beyond anyone's dreams with their mosques and minarets. Furthermore, many Byzantine scholars and philosophers escaped westward, helping to set in motion the tremendous artistic and intellectual ferment we call the Renaissance.

Mehmet's successors, like Selim the Grim, a leader inflexible in the pursuit of enemies or justice, gave the Turk his terrible bad name.

Ottoman armies under Sulayman reached the gates of Vienna before they were turned back. "Grass never grows where a Turk's horse has trod" became a sad but true Balkan proverb, and Balkan mothers used to scare their children when they were bad, by threatening, "If you keep on being bad, the Terrible Turk will get you!"

Actually the "Terrible Turk" was no worse than his neighbors. After more than one victory Christian leaders like the Hungarian Hunyadi boasted of having taken no prisoners. Treaties were seldom honored; in fact the Serbs broke one solemn peace by a surprise raid which led to their worst defeat, the battle of Kossovo. It was the temper of the times. Besides, the Ottomans lived for many years in close contact with the cultured Byzantines and Selcuks; the Emperor Manuel enjoyed the hospitality of their court in exile; their ancient capital of Bursa is full of beautiful works of art, all purely Ottoman.

Furthermore the Ottoman permitted Christians to keep their religion, if they accepted the *political* authority of Islam. They were much more tolerant of the Christian peasantry than the Byzantine emperors had been, and there was little interference with their private lives.

Mehmet Fatih conquered Constantinople, but in time and with a persistence worthy of his own people, the city and its Byzantine atmosphere, with a subtle alchemy, altered forever the simple character of the Turks. Decades of exposure to civilization had already smoothed their barbarian rough edges; now the elaborate rituals and institutions of the old Empire were taken over by its new owners. It is said that Mehmet's respect for Constantinople was so great that when he first entered the city after its capture and found one of his men breaking up the pavement in front of Santa Sophia, he gave the man one hundred lashes on the spot. Then he ordered the church of churches to be turned into a mosque. Mehmet also realized that he needed the cooperation of the Greek population to run Istanbul, and he had one of their monks, George Scholarius, invested as Gennadios II, Patriarch of the Greek Orthodox Church, to take charge of their affairs. This was the start of the millet system, one of the unique features of government contributed by the Ottomans, about which we shall hear more later.

When we think of Turks, we still have a well-conditioned reflex which associates them with harems, beautiful slave girls, eunuchs, sumptuous feasts where diners recline on couches to watch veiled dancers, and such things. Originally none of these were Turkish; the Ottomans borrowed them from the Byzantines. Thus the Byzantine Emperor had several wives, although one was always the Queen, and many concubines; he kept these secluded in a series of rooms called the *gynacaeum*. They did not wear veils, but were just as unavailable to the man in the street as the veiled harem women. The Emperor was identified in Greek Orthodox rituals as Jesus' representative on earth, and venerated as someone divine; if you wanted an audience with him, you entered on hands and knees, kissed his foot, and crawled out backwards. The Ottoman Sultan was also Caliph of Islam, and demanded exactly the same veneration.

No doubt in time the Ottomans would have lost their Central Asian vigor just as all ruling peoples seem to, after considerable exposure to civilization and its luxuries. The inevitable decline of their military and administrative power, however, was due as much to their administrative system as to their establishment in the Byzantine capital. This curious administrative setup was useful in the beginning, but like every administration, it needed to change with changing times. The civilized world which the Ottomans entered was a medieval world; people believed in miracles, in charms, and attached marvelous powers to alleged relics of early Christianity such as a piece of wood from the True Cross. But the Ottomans stayed in a medieval world, and meanwhile Europe entered the modern world. There is a parallel between the Ottoman Empire and the Russian Empire of the Czars, its worst enemy. In both the gulf between classes was enormous; an Anatolian peasant farmer had no more in common with a fat Istanbuli pasha than did a Russian *moujik* with a Muscovite *boyar*. In both empires religion was closely tied with the state, and the conservative religious leaders, priests or *mullahs,* opposed any changes. Not until the twentieth century did these two empires begin to become modernized.

The Ottoman administration invented certain institutions which worked very well while the sultans were able men and a few Turks were in control of large numbers of foreigners. The most important of these institutions, in terms of future consequences to the empire, was the Capitulations. The rulers of Constantinople had from time to time given special privileges to trading merchants from other states, like the Republics of Venice and Genoa; the Genoese merchants had their own special quarter of the city under their flag. In 1521 the Ottomans resumed the practice and reconfirmed Venetian privileges in a treaty listing these privileges in thirty chapters (Latin *capitula*). Sulayman the Magnificent signed a similar treaty with France in 1536, much to England's horror that a Christian nation should make any alliance with a Moslem one. (England was to do the same a few years later.) These Capitulations pleased the Turks because they encouraged trade; it was also a way for them to show how generous they were to the "inferior" Christian states. Besides, they disliked commercial transactions; it was much simpler for them not to bother with business details, and leave commerce to the "inferiors." Each Capitulatory treaty began with the preamble: "Graciously accorded by the Sultan, ever victorious, to the infidel king of ———, ever vanquished."

According to the Capitulations, the citizens receiving them did not have to pay Ottoman taxes, or obey Ottoman laws, but were subject to the laws and taxes of their *own* country. They could only be arrested by their own ambassadors. Ottoman policemen could enter their homes or businesses only by invitation. The system was workable while the Christian nations were weak and Turkey strong, but it began to boomerang when the reverse came into effect. Istanbul in the nineteenth century had more shyster lawyers, confidence men, and crooks of all kinds than any other city in the world; people escaping from justice in their own countries used to find perfect safety there. Meanwhile the sultans, their treasuries empty, were forced to borrow at ruinous rates from their former "inferiors."

By the nineteenth century Ottoman Turkey was so corrupt that a few more shysters or usurers made little difference. A Russian tsar coined the phrase "The Sick Man of Europe" for the dying empire. Here and there were bright spots and revivals—a few good sultans, reform-minded prime ministers—but conservative reactionary elements were too strong. The average Anatolian farmer was farther removed from his government than in the worst days of Arab raids; he was over-taxed and dragged off without choice to fight and die on distant fields. One wonders how such a brave and energetic people, simple, realistic, good soldiers and administrators, could sink so low.

Another institution which began well and ended badly was the millet system. When Mehmet Fatih named Gennadius Patriarch, he made the Greek bishop the steward of his people; that is, the Sultan left the Greeks of Istanbul to run their own affairs, as long as they paid a poll tax and behaved themselves. The millet was both national and religious. "People of the Book" (i.e. Christians and Jews, because each had a "Book" of religious and social guidance) were members of different millets; the Jews were one, and Christians were divided according to sect, as Armenians, Georgian Christians, Egyptian Copts, etc. In cases of disputes between members of a millet the chief magistrate, and not the Sultan, made the final decision. The Ottomans themselves were a millet, the ruling group of Islam.

Although non-Moslem millets were in theory second-class citizens, having to pay a poll tax and not being allowed to carry arms or serve in the Ottoman armies, there were certain advantages to the system for them from the start. Since they operated most of the Empire's commercial ventures anyway, it was expedient for the proud Turks to treat them decently. There are instances of the Sultan interfering to protect a millet from its own magistrate; thus Murad IV ordered in 1640 that a certain Armenian bishop stop taking his cut from the collection plate and levying a fruit tax on his people for the orchards attached to his church. The millet also kept alive the spirit of nationalism among these defeated peoples, and it was much easier for them to revolt against the weakening Ottoman rule in the nineteenth century. Finally, the exemption from military service deprived the Sultan of an excellent source of manpower.

Another important institution which proved harmful for the Ottomans was the Janissary system. It was originally a personal bodyguard of the Sultan composed of Christians captured in war and converted to Islam. According to old traditions the Sultan was allowed one fifth of all the loot taken in campaigns for his personal use. The best and strongest Christians taken prisoner were part of this one fifth, and were assigned to his bodyguard as "new troops"—Yeni Cheri, in Turkish, corrupted into English as janissary.

When the Sultan's wars began to bring fewer captives, the Ottomans began a conscription, possibly the first in history. Teams of recruiting officers would visit a Balkan village, pick the most suitable boy between eight and twelve, and haul him off to Istanbul. There he was converted to the Moslem faith, in a ceremony which he seldom understood, and from that day on was the property of the state. He could not marry (this rule was changed later); he received rigorous, spartan training; he learned perfect discipline and obeyed his leaders without question. In return he held a privileged position in the imperial court and the army. No rank except that of sultan itself, reserved to male members of the house of Osman, was closed to him; he could rise higher in imperial service than any born Moslem.

These advantages made membership in the Janissary Corps an honor which was eagerly sought after by Moslem subjects of the Empire. In battles the janissaries were the last line of defense. There is a story of a troop of French knights who attacked a larger Ottoman army, and cut their way gloriously through four lines of defense, slaughtering Turks as they went. When they reached the top of a little hill and thought they had finished their opponents, they were appalled to see the six-thousand-strong Janissary Corps lined up waiting for them. All the

French were so horrified that they threw down their weapons and ran. On another occasion a janissary was leading a group of prisoners from one town to another. He discovered that he had left his gear behind. Leaving his sword with the prisoners, he warned them to stay where they were, on pain of death, until he returned. Only one of the prisoners took the opportunity and escaped—he was the one who lived to tell the story. Such was the reputation of the janissaries.

In time the Janissary Corps became corrupt and bloodthirsty. Life was too easy for them. They made and unmade sultans. According to their mood. When janissaries wished to show their dislike of a sultan, they overturned the kettledrums which they carried into battle; at this point the sultan would very quickly agree to their demands. Finally, in 1826, they did this for the last time; the new sultan, Mahmud II, was ready for them. He had secretly built up his own army, and those janissaries he did not shoot down were blown up in their own barracks.

The last two hundred and fifty years of the Ottoman Empire were a sad story which the modern Turks would like to forget. They prefer to look farther back in time, to the Empire's heyday; one of the biggest celebrations in recent years was the five hundredth anniversary, on May 29, 1953, of the capture of Constantinople. Practically everybody in modern Istanbul was dressed either as a janissary or as a sultan! Great days were revived, and forgotten were such horrible institutions as the wholesale slaughter by each new sultan of all his brothers, to protect his own right to the throne.

When this system endangered the succession, the sultans developed an equally horrible method. This was the *kafes* (cage). When a sultan died all his sons were taken to an enclosed area within the palace, and except for the one who inherited the throne, they stayed in this "cage" for the rest of their lives. Sometimes a prince with many years to his credit in the kafes became sultan by chance or default; these sultans, if not completely mad from the experience, were generally unfit to rule an empire. The system was a vicious spiral; a sultan weakened by years of virtual imprisonment came out, and sired weak sons who were in turn confined and further weakened. Although much depended upon the length of confinement, it is somewhat of a miracle that any sound men ruled the Empire while the kafes was in use. In the late nineteenth century nonruling princes were given a great deal more freedom, but by then it was too late.

The incredible thing is that the Empire and the ruling house of Osman (remember it was the only family to rule) were tolerated and actually obeyed for so long after both began to decline. But the people of Anatolia not only tolerated but supported the sultans. The Anatolians were the backbone of the Empire as they had been of Byzantium, and were no better off—overtaxed, oppressed, conscripted to fight on distant frontiers without pay, and called Turks, in scorn, to distinguish them from the lordly and ruling Ottomans. But to them the sultan was lord and caliph, or God's deputy on earth in their religion, and they stuck with him.

In 1906 came the first ray of hope for these long-suffering people. The sultan of the time, Abdul Hamid II, had begun his reign in 1876 with promises of a constitution and a reputation for liberal and enlightened thinking. Once secure in his job, he broke his promise, suspended the constitution, dismissed all his advisors, and for thirty years ran what was left of the Empire as an absolute dictator. He had his own spy system, and had spies spying on the spies. He trusted no one; every bite of food had to be tasted by three people before he would eat it. He used to invite possible rivals and leaders of the millets to Istanbul for "visits" which lasted for years. Two events brought about the end of this despot. In 1906 a group of western-minded army officers, called the Young Turks, forced him by a palace revolution to reinstate the 1876 constitution, and then in 1909 he was deposed by the same group.

Unfortunately for Ottoman Turkey these fresh winds blew just a few years too late. The atmosphere of Istanbul, which had corrupted the Byzantines, had corrupted Ottomans from within. Even their language was no longer their own, for Ottoman Turkish was written in Arabic script and had very few Turkish words. One conspicuous lack was a word meaning "interested"; the ruling circles were not *interested* in western technical progress and unable to understand their defeats. The three Young Turks who led Turkey after the sultan's deposition —Enver Pasha, Talaat Pasha, and Jemal Pasha, with their red fezzes, their parade-ground airs were considered a comic trio by Britain and France, and almost in childish reaction, the three led Turkey into the World War I as an ally of Germany. At home they, mostly Enver, ruled as absolutely as had Abdul Hamid. Their military rashness (especially Enver's, as chief of staff) led to defeat after defeat; only at Gallipoli, where Mustapha Kemal served, did the Turkish armies show well. The war's end saw Ottoman Turkey prostrate under Allied occupation. Only a new Gray Wolf could revive the Turks.

4. Out of the Ashes

IN 1919 AND 1920 the victorious Allies of World War I —Great Britain and France, with Italy and Greece tagging along, occupied Anatolia. A British cruiser dropped anchor off Istanbul and British and French troopers began standing guard over the Sultan. The French general even rode into the city on a white horse, in ironic memory of Sultan Mehmet Fatih's entry in 1453. Italian forces took over areas in the south, and the Greeks landed at Smyrna. Even the Armenians, out in eastern Turkey, showed their independence; their delegation to the Peace Conference with the defeated Germans received a promise of an Armenian republic. This division of the last portion of the Ottoman Empire was in accordance with various secret agreements made between the Allies earlier in the war. Only one small section of Anatolia was left to the Turks themselves.

At first the Turks seemed to be in no condition to turn defeat into "peace with honor." Those who survived the war—and thousands did not—were gaunt, hungry men and women, without hope for the future. If the Anatolian peasant thought at all about why the Empire had been defeated, he grew bitter about his leaders. He blamed the Sultan, but most of all he blamed Enver Pasha. Enver's military genius had caused thirty-six thousand casualties in the forty-thousand-man Eastern Army in one battle, and Enver had backed a loser by joining forces with Germany. But there was no way to reach Enver; he had gone off to Central Asia to unite the Turks there into a new Turkish Empire, and died in a cavalry charge against the Bolsheviks. So there was nothing to do but pick up what pieces remained of the old life. A few bold spirits took to the hills in the old Akritai tradition, but most of the Sultan's soldiers drifted back to their villages, dejected, many wounded, nearly all unpaid.

This was certainly Ottoman Turkey's darkest hour, the hour of national shame. The "Sick Man" lay on his deathbed. But in this darkest hour two things happened that pumped new life into his veins. The first was the arrival of the Greeks. The second was the appearance of a new hero, one who turned his back on the weak Ottomans and brought new confidence to the downtrodden, long-forgotten Turks of Anatolia.

The Turks did not object when Britons, Frenchmen, and Italians took over their territory; they had no choice anyway. But when the Greeks, their former subjects, occupied Smyrna and began moving east to add more territory to the new "Greek Empire of Constantinople," even the long-suffering Anatolians became angry. A Greek recapture of Anatolia after six hundred years was an insult. Bands of Turks began to harass the Greek forces; they were no match for the regular Greek army but at least they were able to pick off Greeks here and there. Still it was obvious that Turkey needed a new Gray Wolf.

Fortunately one was waiting in the wings, a military hero who could lead and administrate and make even personal enemies, in this land of family feuds, cooperate. His name was Mustafa, and he was the son of a customs inspector in Salonika (now part of Greece but at that time still in Ottoman hands). Against his mother's wishes he attended military school, where a teacher named Kemal took a fancy to him. So the bright young Mustafa became Mustafa Kemal, and eventually Mustafa Kemal Ataturk, the "Father of the Turks." He had made a name for himself early as a brilliant soldier, but he was also mixed up in various secret societies that were plotting to overthrow the Sultan and modernize Turkey, and had the reputation of being independent-minded. Several times he was lucky to escape with his life from Abdul Hamid's spies, and the general staff shipped him off to distant command posts to keep him out of trouble.

When the World War I broke out the Ottoman Empire needed every bit of military talent it could find, and Mustafa Kemal came back from the provinces. His most important campaign was on the Gallipoli Peninsula, where an invasion army of British and Anzac troops tried to capture the Straits. Largely through his brilliant leadership the ragged Turkish army fought the invaders to a draw. Mustafa Kemal also saved another Turkish army from a trap in Syria. But these successes, if you can call them that, made the sultan and the generals jealous of him. At the end of World War I, the sultan packed him off to Anatolia as inspector-general of the eastern armies.

As things turned out, this was the best possible move for Mustafa Kemal. It shows the ostrich-like thinking of the Ottomans. They loved intrigue and plot; they also held the greatest scorn for the people of their Anatolian provinces. There were really two worlds in the dying Ottoman Empire, one the luxurious corrupt court of Constantinople, the other the poor run-down peasantry of Anatolia. Yet Mustafa Kemal understood the virtues of the much-maligned Turks, and realized that a Turkish revival would have to take place away from Constantinople.

He was posted to Samsun, a Black Sea port on Turkey's north shore. There the luck which held for him throughout his life was in evidence. He discovered that the people of Anatolia were very angry— angry over defeat, angry over occupation, angry about their do-nothing Sultan, and angriest of all about the Greek invasion. The courtiers in Constantinople knew nothing of this discontent. Mustafa Kemal went straight to work. He organized the discontented Turks into nationalist committees, and began to form an army from his headquarters at Angora (now Ankara). Most important, he set up supply lines overland from Inebolu to Angora for vital equipment stolen or smuggled from Constantinople under the noses of the occupation forces.

The story of Turkey's war of independence has been told many times. Probably the best authorities on it are the people who took part in it. If you will put yourself in the shoes of these people, people like Halide Edib, the first Turkish woman to graduate from a European college, her husband Dr. Adīvar, Colonel Ismet Pasha, later Inönü, or Mustafa Kemal himself, you'll be able to understand Turkey's remarkable progress in thirty-five years. These people started with literally nothing, no roads, no military weapons except old rifles, no communications, no industry. They even had to fight against the Sultan's own armies. We are not surprised any more when a nation becomes independent, but we ought to remember that Turkey was the first to do so in this century, and without becoming a dictatorship, too.

The Turkish nationalists were further handicapped by having to fight on two fronts. One front was against enemy armies occupying Anatolia. French troops had control in Cilicia, the British held Constantinople and Thrace (the last Ottoman possession in Europe which had also been the first, six hundred years earlier), the Italians were in command on the south and southeast coasts. The Sultan's own armies soon declared Mustafa Kemal a rebel, and moved inland against his ragtag army. But the worst blow to nationalist prestige was delivered by the Greeks. With British encouragement and a specific promise of Anatolian territory from Prime Minister Lloyd George, two Greek armies landed at Smyrna and began pushing toward Angora.

The second front was social, not military; although you could see traces of it everywhere, it was very hard to overcome. It was the battle of liberation from the dead hand of the past. After six centuries of Ottoman rule the people of Anatolia, themselves Turks, were so downtrodden and degraded that their very name was a synonym for "boorish peasant." Hardly a single new idea had developed in the Empire in centuries; while Europe was having its Renaissance and Industrial Revolution, the Turks stagnated. Centuries of defeat had robbed the Turks of their self-respect, and years of neglect turned the rich wooded land of Anatolia into a barren waste, studded with tiny villages cut from rock escarpments or built of mud bricks that disintegrated in the rain, with a population ignorant of realities except for death, the daily toil, and the Ottoman tax collector.

We often find examples in history of a whole nation reawakening under the noses of its reactionary rulers, who do not see the significance of what is happening until it is too late and they have lost their jobs and thrones. While the sultan twiddled his thumbs in Constantinople, and Ottoman officials danced with foreign ladies at fancy-dress balls night after night, the young Turkish officers joined Mustafa Kemal. The government might not care what happened to Turkey, but they did! And it was obvious to most of them that the Allies intended to cut up the Empire into little pieces, unless the Turks could prove by actions that they could run their own affairs.

During the days of the occupation, then, these young Turkish officers went unobtrusively about their business, holding ordinary civilian or military jobs. Many of them were from the best families in Constantinople; their fathers, rich landowners, bankers, even army generals, remained fanatically loyal to the Sultan, ready to execute anyone who collaborated with "that renegade" Mustafa Kemal. But danger on three sides—from the Allied occupation troops, the Sultan's soldiers, and their own fathers—did not stop the young officers. Late each night, when their families were in bed, they left their homes, clad in gray wool sweatsuits and tennis shoes. Noiselessly they crept through the narrow streets to the arsenals, loaded rifles, ammunition, even dismantled artillery, in carts, and took these to the waterfront. There the equipment was smuggled on board ships bound for Inebolu. When, each morning, the freighter nosed through the Bosphorus, the British sentries watching it never guessed that in the hold was a cargo, not of produce, but of live ammunition for the nationalist armies. Nor did they guess that almost half of the aged peasants aboard, wrapped in long cloaks, were young officers going to join those same armies.

The arms lift was just as exciting at the other end. No road ran from Inebolu to Angora, but there was a cart track. Every available means of transport—carts, carriages, and peasant backs—was put into service. Young Mehmed, riding a horse now, followed the cart track through the flinty hills. He was excited by the prospect of fighting for Turkish independence, and hardly noticed the human chain of peasant women and children carrying weapons down to the army. It had to be this way because all the men were either in Angora or already dead or war prisoners after four bitter years. This human chain even carried cannon, dismantled piece by piece, for nearly three hundred miles in the snow of the winter of 1920. Whole families joined the "foot-lift"; if Mehmed had been watching, he would have seen mothers carrying their babies on their hips, a cartridge belt wrapped around each infant.

When his army was ready, Mustafa Kemal moved. The Sultan kept on playing with his beads, while his ministers denounced the rebel of Angora. The nationalist army was ragged, but it had discipline and a cause to fight for. First it moved against the French armies. The French were defeated in a couple of minor skirmishes but more convincing to them was the siege of the town of Aintab. Twelve thousand French troops surrounded the town, but the handful of defenders, so short of equipment that they used unexploded enemy shells as grenades, held out for ten months before hunger forced them to surrender. Because of this bravery the nationalist government renamed the town Gaziantep, which means Warrior for the Faith. The French decided that Mustafa Kemal was competent to manage their section of occupied Turkey, and that there was no percentage in staying. They were followed by the Italians. Next the Sultan's own troops attacked the rebels, and the government took away Mustafa Kemal's army commission. He beat them to it by resigning. Many of the Ottoman soldiers joined his army. The Greek threat was most serious; the Greeks really intended to increase their territory at Turkish expense. All through 1921 and 1922 the two armies battled, and in September of that year, Mustafa Kemal rode into Smyrna. From their ships in the harbor the survivors of the Greek army looked back at the blazing city, their last toehold in Anatolia. The Greeks had been most successful in 1919 and 1920, when the nationalists were divided and short of equipment. They very nearly won all of western Anatolia at the three-days' battle of the Sakarya River. But Mustafa Kemal issued an order of the day saying that there would be no more retreat; the troops would stay there or die. The Greek army was superior in arms and equipment, but the Turks were fighting for their own land; besides, their leader had told them to stand fast.

Following the Greek departure the nationalists arranged an armistice with the British. Not a shot was fired. By the end of the year Mustafa Kemal had reunited Turkey—a compact, manageable Turkey for the Turks.

In 1923, the Treaty of Lausanne between Turkey and the Allies recognized an independent Turkish state in Anatolia and Western Thrace—exactly what Mustafa Kemal had dreamed of as an officer in the defeated Ottoman army of 1917. To make Turkey literally for the Turks, the Greek population still living in Anatolia was exchanged for the Turkish population of Greece, except for the Greeks of Constantinople, who ran all the businesses and were needed for reconstruction because of their commercial skill, and the Turks of Western Thrace. Turkey gave up all claims to the Ottoman possessions outside Anatolia. The Straits, fought over so bitterly at Gallipoli, were given to Turkey permanently. Thus by 1923 the war on the first front was over.

The war on Turkey's second front took a lot longer to win than the war of liberation from foreign occupation. That second front, you will remember, was against intolerance, outmoded traditions, conservatism, religious bigotry—all the bad qualities that had developed in the late Ottoman Empire. All but a few Turks agreed with Mustafa Kemal on expelling the foreign invaders, but many of them disagreed with him on the need for reforms in society. They had different reasons for disagreeing, depending on their station in life. The rich landowners wanted to keep their lands and revenues; some of the politicians were jealous of Mustafa Kemal's popularity; the ranking officers felt they should be rewarded with lands and big pensions; the priests and peasants were suspicious of a leader who said religion should be separated from the state. Also a number of prominent nationalists resented his dictatorial manner, although they admitted that he was usually right and acted for the good of the country.

Even though he was the man of the hour, Mustafa Kemal had to move slowly and carefully in his reforms. The ones which would arouse least opposition, naturally, came first. The Turkish capital was moved officially to Ankara. Because of the Sultan's disgraceful behavior in giving in to the peace terms which partitioned Ottoman Turkey, and sending an army to fight the nationalists, it was not too difficult for the Grand National Assembly to agree to eliminate the Sultan. The job was abolished, and the last member of the House of Osman, Mehmed VI Vahdettin, left Constantinople hastily at night on a British warship. The official change of name from Constantinople to Istanbul completed the break with the Ottoman (and incidentally Byzantine) past.

The next problem was to establish a republican form of government and begin educating the Turks for democracy. This was much harder than it might seem now. The peasants were reasonably democratic in their villages, but they were used to a strong autocratic government which did their thinking for them. They were also used to a chief executive who was head of their religion—for the Sultan had been Caliph (the pope of Islam) since the sixteenth century. Again Mustafa Kemal moved slowly. He worked privately to win a majority of delegates to the Assembly to his plans, and then the provisional government which had been running Turkey resigned. It was impossible for the Assembly to agree on a new cabinet, and a committee went to see Mustafa Kemal at his house in Çankaya, a suburb of Ankara. He of course had been waiting for this opportunity. He went to the Assembly, and told the deputies that their trouble was in the old Constitution of 1906, which was still in effect. He said he proposed to amend it. There was a great hullabaloo at this, but everybody soon understood the sense of the amendments he offered, for they specified that Turkey belonged to the Turks, and should therefore be a republic. The amendment was approved, a new constitution adopted, and Mustafa Kemal became first President of Turkey.

His purpose in his fifteen years in office was to make Turkey into a modern European state, progressive and free of all reactionary or foreign influences. To make such a change in a country made up of peasants, defeated in war, bankrupt, mostly illiterate, with no knowledge of the modern industrial world, he was forced to become a dictator. Mustafa Kemal was the sort of man who would brook no opposition to his ideas anyway. It is to his credit, nonetheless, that he refused to be treated as a god, and encouraged opposition so long as it contributed to Turkey's healthy progress.

With the Sultan out of the way, the next logical departure was the Caliph. "Why do we need a caliph?" Mustafa Kemal asked. "We are a republic; this means every man has a right to his own religion, and to practice it as he wishes. Do we ask other men to tell us how to eat, how to pray, what to wear on our heads and bodies, how much to give to charity, how to make wills, kill sheep during holidays, treat our wives? No, we do not. Yet we allow the Caliph to do just that; and the Caliph is not God, he is a man." The logic was unanswerable, and the office of Caliph was abolished. This step aroused much opposition and even fighting; many people felt it was sacrilegious. The *ulema* (Islamic clergy) were furious at the prospect of losing their prestige, and the dervishes thought the country would be visited with hellfire and damnation. But a year after the end of the caliphate, the Turks had forgotten it.

The most interesting of Mustafa Kemal's reforms were in names and dress. Until his time all Turks had had only one name, their first name. In order to distinguish one Ahmed or Mehmed from thousands of others, he would also carry his father's name, and usually an adjective describing him or his place of birth. Thus you might have Mehmed son of Ahmed the carriage maker, or Ahmed from Sivas, or Ismet with the big nose. Mustafa Kemal decreed that everybody should take a last name. To start things off the Assembly gave him the surname

Ataturk (father of the Turks). General Ismet took the surname Inönü, after the place where he had defeated the Greeks. There was vast confusion for a time, as people hunted through dictionaries, telephone books, or libraries, to find interesting or colorful last names.

The traditional Turkish fez was next to go. The fez was a more difficult problem than European clothing to sell to the Turkish public. It is a brimless round, almost conical cap, either with or without a tassel, and still worn in Arab countries. Moslem men are supposed to wear headgear of some sort, and the lack of a brim permits the wearer to keep his hat on while touching his forehead to the floor at prayers in the mosque. Ataturk considered it just one more symbol of the hold which reactionary Islamic customs had over the Turks, and he was determined to eliminate it. He started wearing a soft panama hat in the summer. Next he and a group of his officials went to Kastamonu, a town famous for its conservative attitudes. He and his party wore hats. He told a horrified crowd of Kastamonu-ites, "I've brought you some nice presents. They are called hats. . . . They are much more suitable than the fez as a protection against the sun and the rain." If this seems amusing to you, remember that in Anatolia the phrase "şapka giymek," which means literally "to put on a hat," had the idiomatic meaning "to give up your religion." So Ataturk's determined attack on the fez took courage even for him.

Again, he was right, and everyone had to accept his arguments. After all, he pointed out, the fez was not Turkish, but had been borrowed from the Venetian to replace the equally unsuitable turban, and that it was unnecessary to wear a hat at all to mosque. Eventually a law prohibited the fez, but it caused no trouble, for Ataturk had laid the necessary groundwork.

The only reform of Ataturk's which was unsuccessful was the removal of the veil. Turkish women, like all Moslem women, for centuries went out in public (if at all) wearing a *yaşmak,* a shapeless black sack of a garment, and a veil. They did this because the Koran, the Islamic Bible, said that women were inferior to and dependent on men, although permitting them to own property and because custom decreed that women should be decorous and behave modestly in public. Thus if Ataturk had tried to pass a law forbidding veils, he would have had to fight all the irate husbands in Turkey as well as the ordinary reactionaries. So he let nature take its course. The women of Anatolia had been his strongest supporters in the War of Independence. Many of them already believed that women should have more rights and privileges. Education did the rest. In the towns and cities, women shucked off their veils almost as soon as they were allowed to vote (which, by the way, was before American women were). In the back-country of Anatolia, even today, a woman is apt to hide her face from a stranger, or fold a scarf across the lower part of her face. Old men who grew up under the sultans sometimes say of a woman they dislike that "she would look better behind the veil than in front of one," but they are in the minority.

Ataturk put a great deal of emphasis on education, of course. Turkey was about ninety per cent illiterate when the Republic started; today it is about seventy per cent literate. American-founded colleges such as Robert College in Istanbul did a great deal of training, especially in science and engineering, of young Turks, but it always had a small enrollment and limited budget. The Ottomans had never had an American-style university with graduate and undergraduate faculties; the Republicans established one at Istanbul, another at Ankara, and more recently Eğe University at Izmir. Ataturk University, to serve the needs of this most backward section of Turkey, mainly in agriculture and vocational education, is being established at Erzurum in eastern Anatolia. This will give the Republic four institutions of higher learning, plus a technical institute at Istanbul.

Even more significant has been the progress in secondary education since Ataturk's start in the 1920's. Most villages had no school at all then, and all teaching was done by the *hocas,* who trained the boys (no girls) to recite the Koran by heart. Ataturk promoted the establishment of Village Institutes, where future teachers were instructed for five years and then sent to remote areas to start their own schools. In this way Turks helped to educate themselves.

The most entertaining of Ataturk's many reforms in Turkish life was the language reform. The first Turks arrived in Anatolia speaking a simple, forceful language—the language of the camp, the tent, the horse, the cavalry skirmish. Once in a while this early Turkish speech attained some of the dignity and beauty of pure poetry; unfortunately the Ottomans soon found its vocabulary ill-suited to the demands of governing an empire. Being imitative, they quickly adopted Arabic and the Arabic alphabet as the most useful language of government. They were also strongly influenced by Persian culture, and many Persian words were found useful to their administration. The common people went on speaking Turkish (or whatever their native tongue happened to be), but they had to write it in Arabic script, from right to left. They had a terrible time, since Turkish has eight vowels and Arabic only three. The Ottoman court developed its own method of communication, a language written in Arabic and composed of more Arabic and Persian words than Turkish. Communication between the government and the ordinary Turks was often difficult, Ottoman Turkish being full of flowery phrases which confused people who asked simple questions which required direct answers. This explains in part why the Ottomans used the word Turk to refer to an ignorant, ill-mannered fellow, and liked to call themselves Ottomans, or Osmanlis. It also explains the decline of their empire; Ottoman officials kept their positions not by merit so much as by retiring behind a screen of polite doubletalk that protected them from taking action on any matter unless they really had to.

In order to break this linguistic stranglehold on Turkey, Ataturk resorted to the direct method. He called a conference of scholars and asked them how long it would take to teach the country to use Turkish in a Latin alphabet, much more suitable to the language than Arabic because of the vowel problem. The scholars came up with an estimate of fifteen years. "Very well," he said, "you have six months."

At the end of this six-month period, one morning, all the newspapers in Istanbul were published in Turkish, written from left to right as we do, in Latin script. Many people were horrified; many could not read the papers that day, or for weeks thereafter. The clergy raged; the Koran, God's word transmitted through Mohammed, was in Arabic, they said. So Ataturk took chalk and a blackboard, and stumped the countryside. In every village he visited, he set up his blackboard under the plane trees and conducted classes in the "New Turkish." "The best proof that we are Turks," he said, "is that we have our own national language." After a while even the patriarchs, smoking their nargiles (bubble-pipes) in the coffeehouses, came over to listen and be instructed. Ataturk had succeeded again, by positive, dynamic action, in pushing ahead on the road to modern civilization.

Mustafa Kemal Ataturk died on November 10, 1938. One way to measure what he meant to his people can be shown by their behavior when his death was announced. An entire nation of stolid, reserved, disciplined, unemotional people, broke down and wept. Thousands of crying men, women, even children, followed his coffin from Istanbul to the train for Ankara, its last resting place. The moment of his death is still celebrated each year by a minute of silence, all over Turkey.

It may seem strange that these same Turks who felt so emotionally about their first leader, and who hang his picture in every public place, would vote against the political party he founded. But that is exactly what happened twelve years after his death. Ataturk made enemies during his career, of course; he was too bold and confident, and sure of the rightness of his policies to avoid this. However, as he himself said, "I will lead my people by the hand until they can walk alone. Then my work will be done." When he died the Turkish people were surprised to find his example had given them the strength they needed to walk unaided. The Grand National Assembly, without a dissenting vote, chose Ismet Inönü as the new President. The first President's advice to his people—"Çaliş! Güven! Oğun!" (Work! Be Confident!

Be Proud!)—was carried on without deviation during the difficult war years and the first decade of the Cold War.

Turkey's first opposition political party was formed in 1946 by four of Ataturk's followers: Celal Bayar, a banker and early nationalist rebel, Adnan Menderes, an American-educated (in Smyrna) and independently wealthy landowner, Refik Koraltan, a lawyer, and Fuad Köprülü, a descendant of a great family of Grand Viziers in the Ottoman Empire and Turkey's leading scholar. They called themselves the Democrat party. At first they didn't amount to much, but the fact that President Inönü allowed them to function at all showed that Turkey was "walking alone." Finally, in 1950, Turks went to the polls in the country's first free, secret election. Resentment over high prices, low salaries, food shortages, etatism (Ataturk's policy of state control of industry), wicked taxes (all blamed on the Republicans but not on Ataturk) produced a complete reversal of the expected results; the Democrats won by a landslide. Celal Bayar became President, Adnan Menderes Prime Minister. In 1954 and 1957 they were re-elected.

The problems which Turkey's new government has faced since 1950 would have taxed the abilities of any leader, even Mustafa Kemal. The price of freedom, of maintaining a large army for defense against possible Russian aggression (and the Turks have fought too many wars against Russia to make any distinction between Russia and Communism), has been high. Over one fourth of the Turkish budget each year goes for national defense. Turkey also sent a brigade to Korea during the "police action" there, in answer to a United Nations' request for an international army; this brigade compiled an enviable record for courage under fire. Turkish prisoners, too, showed the strength of their convictions and their determined loyalty to Western ideas; no Turkish captive was successfully brainwashed by the Chinese. Thus although Turkey has not engaged in a major war since the Ottoman defeat in 1918 (she was neutral until the last days of World War II), the traditional Turkish warlike, courageous spirit, is again evident.

We Americans first became interested in Turkey in 1947, when we needed allies against Stalin. The Truman Doctrine began a program of American aid to Turkey that is still going on, and has transformed the country. The Democratic government has generally used this aid wisely, although often criticized for trying to do too many things at once, causing inflation and shortages.

Now morning has come to Anatolia. Far behind us are the minarets and domes of Turkey's Ottoman past; ahead are the square modern buildings of the new capital. The sun is just rising. For the real contrast between the bankrupt battered Empire of 1919 and the vigorous young Republic begins in Ankara.

5. Ataturk's City

NKARA!

The Simplon-Orient Express, now far indeed from Paris, eases into the platforms of a long gray stone railroad station. Its engineer gives two blasts of that high, haunting whistle peculiar to European trains —a whistle that can be as terrifying in the vast silence of an Anatolian night as the howl of a wolf. The doors of the *wagons-lits* open; passengers in a hurry step out, as the baggagemen begin handing down suitcases to the crowd of *hamals*. Just outside the ring of hamals, men in felt caps begin shouting, "Taksi!" A man gets down from one of the rear cars, and is immediately surrounded by a great crowd of Turks. They put a wreath of flowers around his neck, hoist him on their shoulders, and carry him off, shouting and singing, as if he were a successful gladiator in ancient Rome. "A deputy," someone mutters. This is the usual Turkish way of greeting political leaders. But now our bags have been collected; the taxi is waiting. It carries us along wide asphalt streets, their sidewalks and boulevard islands planted with trees and huge pansy beds, to our hotel. What a beautiful, modern, well-planned city this seems to be!

The extraordinary thing is that all this modern beauty is thirty-odd years old. When Ataturk came to Ankara in 1920 to found a new capital, he found literally nothing here. He and his officers rode down a rough cart track into a plain shaped like a rough saucer surrounded by barren hills. In the center of this saucer were two low, steep hills, covered with houses, one fortified with irregular walls. The rest of the plain was empty, except for a few flocks of sheep and goats grazing and the shabby huts of sheepherders. Ankara was a sleepy village of a few thousand souls, situated at the intersection of the main north-south and east-west trade routes across Anatolia. The dribble of trade still being carried across these routes kept Ankara in existence. It was also the end of the German-built rail line from Constantinople, and during World War I received a certain amount of business from troops on their way to the Eastern Front to fight Czarist Russia. But the original reason for building a town there—those in possession of the Angora citadel could control the trade routes—had long been forgotten as the Ottoman Empire decayed.

Why did Ataturk choose this insignificant town in the desolate center of Anatolia as his starting point for New Turkey? His first reason was its location. It was far enough from Constantinople to be out of reach of the Sultan's army and the occupation forces. The cutting of the railroad line isolated Ankara even more. Second, by posting guards at strategic points around the Ankara plain and along the two main trade routes, Ataturk was in a position to block any surprise attacks (remember that the Allies thought his activities were a big joke at first). But Ataturk had more reasons than just military ones for moving to Ankara. The town was in the middle of Anatolia, and he realized that a Turkish revival would have to occur in this most backward part of the Empire, if at all. Also, Ankara had its roots in the pre-Turkish past. Its insignificance was recent. Originally founded by the Phrygians, it was an important provincial capital under the Romans, a Byzantine fortress, a Selcuk citadel, and a key Ottoman trading center as late as the seventeenth century.

The name Ankara memorialized one of the few defeats suffered by the early Ottomans. In the late years of the fourteenth century Sultan Beyazit I, nicknamed *Yildirim* (Lightning) was storming up and down Anatolia and the Balkans, winning new territories for the expanding Ottoman Empire. Nothing remained to the Byzantines by 1400 except

Constantinople, and it seemed only a matter of time before Beyazit would take the city. Then suddenly a Tartar horde led by Tamerlane (Timur-with-the-lame-leg) whirled out of Central Asia into eastern Anatolia. Beyazit and the Ottoman troops he led turned to meet this new threat. Victory after victory had made Beyazit very cocky; he sent an insulting letter to Tamerlane, and strung up Tartar messengers by their ears. In the summer of 1402, the Turks came to Angora. While they were resting in their camp, under the walls of this same citadel, the shadowy Tartar horsemen cut off their water supply and intercepted their food shipments. When the two armies finally met, on a sweltering summer day, the Turks were already beaten. Thousands of them died; Beyazit I was taken prisoner. Christopher Marlowe, an English playwright, says he was carted about in an iron cage until he died, in his play *Tamerlane The Great*. Be that as it may, Tamerlane returned to Central Asia to die, and half a century later Beyazit's great-grandson ruled in Constantinople.

There are really three Ankaras, each with fairly distinct outlines and functions. A frenzied building boom in the capital threatens to absorb many small villages which used to be well outside the city limits; an example is Çankaya, where Ataturk built a summer home where he could retire from the noise and heat of Ankara proper. Çankaya, actually situated on a third low hill in the plain, is a suburb now; so is Bahçelievler (Houses with Gardens), a pretty place to drive around in the spring when the peach trees are in bloom. In fact the general atmosphere of modern Ankara is of a frontier town, a boom town bursting at the seams, rushing to catch up with other world capitals. Except for the lack of night life and saloons, and the corresponding absence of gunplay, you might think you were in a town in the American Wild West. The resemblance is even more marked at sunset. The western section of the saucer flattens out toward Istanbul and the airport, and from all parts of Ankara you can see magnificent sunsets as golden as those on the lone prairie.

This is the atmosphere, the "feel" of Ankara—a city in a hurry, ever

The Mausoleum of Ataturk, where annual ceremonies
commemorate his death, November 10, 1938

The Galata Bridge, Istanbul, looking across
the Golden Horn toward Santa Sophia

Boats taking on cargo at Kadiköy, on
the Asiatic shore opposite Istanbul

Caiques and fishing schooners at anchor in the harbor of Antalya

A village house near Kars, eastern
Turkey, "in the shadow of Mt. Ararat"

A caravan of fig-traders en route to Izmir

The dam at Cubuk, a green oasis supplying Ankara with water

The water detail returning from the village
spring, at Armutlu, on the Gulf of Mudanya

Village girls on their way to school, in Anatolia

One of the wayside fountains built into the wall of
the Gök Medrese, an ancient Selcuk school at Sivas

Inner courtyard of Emirsultan Mosque, Bursa

One of the modern boulevards in Istanbul

Santa Sophia, museum for both Christianity and Islam

The village of Gilindere, on the Mediterranean. Only these houses remain of a flourishing city fifteen hundred years ago.

Stone bridge at Sarikamis, with typical
escarpment houses cut into the cliffs

The Aesculapion, Pergamum, the world's earliest medical center

changing, crude in manners, bedeviled with problems, but dynamic and determined to grow. It is a city like Washington, D.C., in that very few of its inhabitants were born there (excluding the Old City). When the Assembly is in session every hotel is jammed. Delegates from all parts of Turkey crowd tables at the coffeehouses along Ataturk Boulevard to discuss the issues of the day. Then the summer arrives, and all who can rush to Istanbul, leaving the capital and its bracing climate for the sake of crowded apartments along the Bosphorus, and a chance to swim.

The two other main sections of Ankara are Yenişehir (New City) and Ulus (Nation). They are connected by wide Ataturk Boulevard (*Bulvari,* in Turkish). Another wide street, called Mustafa Kemal Bulvari on one side of Ataturk Bulvari and Ziya Gökalp *Caddesi* (Street) intersects on the other Ankara's main street in the form of a T; the point of intersection is called Kīzīlay. Kīzīlay is the heart of Yenişehir. The headquarters of the Turkish Red Crescent Society (Middle Eastern equivalent of our Red Cross) is there; the U.S. Information Service building, called the American Information Center, is half a block up Ataturk Boulevard; the buses from other parts of the city converge there, and such important elements of Ankara life as the Büyük Sinema (Big Movie Theater), Süreyya's night club, the American Library, and the Turkish-American Association are close at hand. Most of the foreign embassies in Ankara are in Yenişehir or its suburb, Kavaklīdere. Except for the Assembly building and a few others, all the important Turkish Government ministries are also in Yenişehir. JUSMMAT (Joint United States Military Mission Aiding Turkey) headquarters sits next to the new Assembly building. So complete is the administrative and accommodation structure in Yenişehir, that many Americans coming to Ankara do not realize that the city has several other sections.

Although quite modern in many respects, Yenişehir has certain odd touches which remind us that it is Turkish. Traffic is not only cars, jeeps, and trucks, but creaking oxcarts and donkeys, herds of cows and flocks of sheep. On the sidewalk in front of the severe white American Embassy a villager is poking a flock of turkeys (the Turks call them *hindi* because they are supposed to have originated in India), along with a stick. The villagers who raise turkeys, if they do not own a truck, must walk their birds many miles overland in order to sell them. This treatment explains why Turkish turkeys are smaller and bonier than the ones you are familiar with. Ankara is not only the national capital, it is a market center and capital of a large province.

Yenişehir is the newest of the "three cities" of Ankara. We put ourselves in the firm hands of a taxi driver who learned his English in Korea, since Ankara has as yet no guide service. He shows us the various ministry buildings, all of a piece since they were designed by the same Austrian architect, Clemens Holzmeister. They are square, functional, six stories high or less (Ankara is in earthquake country), and built of a purplish sandstone with long rows of narrow sash windows that make them seem even more massive. The American Embassy, halfway up the hill to Çankaya, is referred to by its inhabitants as "the White Whale" because of its marble façade; the other embassies occupy older buildings which seem more suited to Turkey than ours.

We soon learn that Yenişehir is not only new, but is changing almost daily, faster than the other sections of Ankara. In fact, there is a story of an American family who went away for the week end and came back to find that their house had been torn down and a three-story apartment building erected on the site! We find that the city is not particularly beautiful, but it takes every possible advantage of its setting. Thus the typical apartment building in Yenişehir is three or four stories, each with a balcony, built at an angle to the street to give the tenants a view of all Ankara from their balconies. The construction is usually concrete or occasionally brick, with red corrugated-tile roofs in the Mediterranean fashion. The floors are often quite beautiful, of marble or terrazzo. The effect from the air of so many identical buildings, each set at an angle to provide the best possible view, is one of confusion and disorder. Yet from a terrace high up in Yenişehir the city is extremely photogenic. The poplars which the "new Turks" planted thirty years ago in this treeless plateau now crisscross in neat rows. A few puffs of smoke in the still air announces the departure of the Erzurum train. The Anit Kabir, or Mausoleum of Ataturk, shines in the clear afternoon air.

Çankaya, at the top of the long hill above Yenişehir, is an interesting village, or rather suburb, since it has been incorporated into greater Ankara. The President of the Republic, Celal Bayar, lives there at the end of Ataturk Boulevard, in a large pink mansion built by and for his predecessors. More interesting than the President's palace, however, is a small house of dark wood with a garden behind it and a pool filled with goldfish. Ataturk built the little house as a retreat. Later he brought his first and only wife, Latife, to live there until they were divorced—the last Moslem divorce in Turkey under the old method, when a man could divorce his wife merely by telling her so. The little chalet is rich in memories of those early years. In the entrance hall is a wall clock stopped at a few minutes after nine A.M.—the time of day of Ataturk's death in 1938. In his study a huge Caucasus bear rug sprawls before his polished ebony desk; an adjoining banquet room holds a long table and sixteen stiff-backed Victorian chairs, where the Turkish Cabinet sat during its all-night deliberations. The rest of the chalet is furnished in the traditional Ottoman manner, with low couches instead of chairs, thick soft rugs handwoven in eastern Turkey, and huge brass *mangals* (a round charcoal brazier with a hinged lid) for heat and cooking. Many of Ankara's houses and apartments still do not have central heating, which in 1920 was nonexistent.

Before driving back down the steep grade to Yenişehir and Ulus, we should stop briefly to take in the view. Below us lies Ankara like a ruffled green velvet rug. There are the two jagged hills of the Old City, the block formation of government buildings, the rows of poplars like soldiers in single file. We can actually see the green creeping outward from the center of this metropolis of nearly half a million now, lapping over gray barren stretches as people put grass and trees around their new houses. The Roman navy got its wood from Anatolia; but all the trees were cut down more than a thousand years ago, and it was said that this part of Anatolia was too dry for agriculture or forestry. Ataturk himself planted trees to prove the doubters wrong. Watching a Turkish gardener at work is an eye-opening experience; Ankara usually has a water shortage in the summer, but Ankarians will go on watering their flowers instead of taking baths—nothing must interfere with proper growth!

Along Ataturk Boulevard between Kızılay and Ulus Square, the center of this part of the capital, are the buildings of the University of Ankara, founded in the 1930's and built of the same gray sandstone as the ministry buildings. Across the street is another small gray building with a bus stop marked "Opera." It is the Ankara Opera House, a perfect gem with a red-gold interior. The Turkish State Opera does a very good job of producing European and American operas in Turkish; recently its lead soprano, Leyla Gencer, made a very successful tour of the United States. Just above the boulevard is the Ethnographical Museum, with a good collection of Turkish folklore—Ataturk's body was kept there until his mausoleum could be completed.

The Assembly still meets in Ulus, on Cumhuriyet Street, in a small yellow building decorated with arches and calligraphy from the old days. But the dominant landmark of Ulus is the equestrian statue of Ataturk in Ulus Square, always called "the Horse's Tail." Traffic converging from half a dozen side streets whirls around the statue. A policeman in white gloves waves his hands furiously. One side of the square is an arcade of little shops, now, unfortunately, very short of goods to display. Still there are hundreds of people strolling, window-shopping, waiting to catch the big German-made buses back to Yeni-şehir.

A French traveler to Ankara in the 1920's, Le Boucher, remarked that "evening activity centers around the statue of Ataturk; everyone, cabinet ministers, deputies, clerks, officers, repairs there to sit and talk furiously about the new Turkey." There is too much motor traffic around the Horse's Tail for people to sit there now, but Ulus is still the center of Turkish life in Ankara. A few doors from the square is Karpiç's, the most famous restaurant in town and for years the only one. The young officers (and their wives as well) from wealthy families in Istanbul, who slipped away to join Ataturk, found the restaurant a relief from cooking on smoky charcoal stoves and a partial cure for their homesickness for the bright lights they had left behind. Ataturk and his cabinet used to come here for eleven-o'clock suppers of *kebab* and *pilav*, and relax a little after long twelve-hour days of patching Turkey together.

Another feature of Ulus, the "middle-aged" of Ankara's three cities, is a large number of buildings with elaborately carved window frames, heavy brass doors, iron grilles over the windows, that look like Oriental palaces. We somehow expect to see princesses looking through the bars. Actually these are banks.

Until 1950 the Government policy was etatism—as has been stated. This actually meant that the state had monopolies over the manufacture and sale of basic commodities, such as sugar, salt, gasoline, and matches, that it controlled food prices, managed the transportation and communications systems, and was responsible for Turkey's industrial development. There was no private enterprise, but the banks that had been in business under the Empire were allowed to continue, and new ones were opened as different parts of the national economy developed. These banks could make loans to individuals; when etatism was abandoned as a total failure and Turkey began to encourage foreign investment and private enterprise, the banks financed many new projects. No one seems to know why the banks look like palaces, when the rest of Ankara is modern and functional. Since we are not in a position to float a loan from a Turkish bank, the only reason for entering one is to change our dollars into Turkish lira. However, the contrast between them and American banks will help you understand something of modern Turkey's administrative problems. Hundreds of clerks, both men and women, sit at open tables or scurry around carrying mysterious notes. The table-sitters take our request for foreign exchange, drop it on a pile of similar ones, and a messenger bears off the entire pile. There are no neat rows of filing cabinets, no apparent order or efficiency, and a topheavy bureaucracy, but eventually we get our liras.

Ankara will never become a tourist attraction on the basis of her ruins, but there are a few points of interest. One is the Temple of Augustus, behind the Ulus Square in a hidden courtyard. All that is left are some crumbled walls and Corinthian columns, but there is an interesting inscription, the Monumentum Ancyranum, which commemorates in Latin the great days of Augustus. You can practice your Latin by reading it.

Nothing is ever wasted in Turkey, and one of the temple walls forms the side wall of the Haci Bayram Mosque, Ankara's holiest. Haci Bayram founded the Bayramī order of dervishes; although the dervish orders are officially outlawed in Turkey, the Turkish attitude is to respect and revere their founders as holy men. If we happen to be in the courtyard on Friday, we will hear the muezzin calling the Moslems of Ankara to prayer, see the faithful crowding into the prayer hall, and listen to Allah's minister chanting *suras* (verses) from the Koran in rich Arabic tones. It is a memorable experience.

Nearby is another small courtyard dominated by a tall marble pillar, the so-called Column of Julian. Julian was the Roman Emperor who became an apostate, that is, he gave up Christianity and tried to restore the old pagan worship of Jupiter, Mars, Venus, and the rest of Olympus. He wasn't very successful, and it may be poetic justice that a pair of storks have built their nest on top of his column, where Julian's statue used to be.

Ulus is somehow a point of transition between the modern quarter of Yenişehir, which we left earlier, and Onculer, the Old City which stood on its two hills when Tamerlane arrived. We can drive part-way up, then we must leave our taxi and struggle up cobbled streets too steep for anything but foot and donkey traffic. We pass girls with jugs of water on their heads which they are carrying to the houses higher on the hillside, since Ankara's permanent water supply does not reach the Old City. The architectural pattern is quite different from that of New Ankara. The houses are packed together, wooden with rough plaster fronts; many have bricks set in the plaster at angles to the horizontal beams, in weird zigzag patterns. There are no balconies, no glass in the windows. On the upper reaches of the two hills the houses are cut in the rock itself, and can be reached only via narrow vertical trails. Many of these rock houses are over a thousand years old. They do not have gardens, although here and there we will see more evidence of the Ankarian's determination to make the desert bloom, in the shape of a few pansies, a peach tree clinging to a crag, or spears of grass being cropped by stubborn Ankara goats.

The cobbled streets of Onculer narrow increasingly toward the top of the Hīdīrlīk, the hill which is crowned by the Selcuk citadel. Inside the citadel itself there is nothing to see except some dusty storerooms and the apartments of the very poor, and in fact the innermost sanctum is locked up. So we have to be satisfied with a look at the walls. These are put together from many periods in history—Ionic columns, Roman and Greek lettering, Selcuk and Ottoman scrollwork, spidery Kufic inscriptions from the Koran, and broken bits of friezes from still earlier periods.

Our driver has an acquaintance named Mehmet who lives inside the citadel, and we stop to see him. He and his family of three live in two rooms just inside the entrance to the citadel. The floor is hard-packed earth; there is neither bathroom nor running water; cooking is done over a small stove that burns kerosene in summer or lignite in winter. Furniture consists of a couple of *kilims* (brightly colored rugs) and cushions. A hard sort of life, we think, yet we are offered tea in demi-tasses, and Mehmet, who works as a *kavass* (doorman) in one of the banks, is terribly proud of his two words of English, Hello, and O.K.

Just outside the walls is a typical Turkish country market, or *pazar*. Modern Ankara's shops have glass fronts and window displays, but in Old Ankara goods are out in plain view, in shops no bigger than a prisoner's cell. Most of the things on sale are staples, for Turkey is not an artistic country in the same way as Italy, for example. Fruits, vegetables in big piles, saddlebags, cooking utensils, household implements, are the rule rather than the exception. Nevertheless several of the streets leading down from the citadel are full of shops which sell the sort of product people like to take home—notably copper trays, brassware, and carpets.

Halfway down the hill from the citadel is the Hittite Museum. We saw earlier the remains of the Hittite capital of Hattusas, near Boğazköy; Hittite culture has become important to present-day Turkey. Another of Ataturk's methods of reviving Turkish nationalism was to sell the idea that the modern Turk was a direct descendant of the once-powerful Hittites. He encouraged archaeological exploration in the various Hittite centers as they were discovered, and imported European archaeologists to train Turks. Such great scholars as John Garstang, Helmut Th. Bossert, and Seton Lloyd, all came to Turkey to work on the Hittite remains. What they and their Turkish colleagues found (at least everything movable) was brought to Ankara and exhibited in two converted buildings side by side. Even if you are opposed to museums by nature, you will be enchanted by Ankara's Hittite exhibition. The main building used to be a caravansaray, a sort of medieval motel for camel caravans and horsemen; it has a very high domed roof and small windows like beehive openings near the top. Two gigantic Hittite warriors in stone are the "doormen." The other building was a *bedesten,* a Turkish market; it has four vaulted arcades around a central open courtyard. Both are full of crudely drawn but bold friezes, and cases of beautiful gold ornaments.

It is a long distance in time from the "night dwellers," those people who erect shacks of tin cans and flattened oil drums up in Onculer, and from the Hittite friezes, to the modern establishments and wide boulevards of new Ankara. We leave the Old City with a sense of having stepped out of the Middle Ages. It doesn't seem possible that there can be a common bond between Old and New Ankara, or between the Onculer women who hide their faces behind their shawls when we pass, and their smartly dressed sisters down on Ataturk Boulevard. But there is. We find this bond in a visit to the Anit Kabir, the Tomb of Ataturk.

The first mausoleum of importance in the world was built for King Mausolus of Halicarnassus, a Greek city on the Aegean coast of this same Anatolia. The word meant "tomb of Mausolus," and now refers to an elaborate tomb. The Mausoleum of Ataturk is the second of its kind, in Anatolia. The Mausoleum of Halicarnassus has long since crumbled, but Ataturk's Mausoleum seems likely to endure as long as Turkey endures. It crowns a small hill on the edge of Yenişehir; only the citadel overtops it. The hill used to be treeless, but evergreens were brought from the four corners of Turkey to be planted as a green border around the rectangular building of orange-colored stone. Impressive rather than beautiful, severe and brooding, it seems already to have lost its newness and become part of the somber landscape of Anatolia. Construction began in 1942, and in November, 1953, the fifteenth anniversary of Ataturk's death, his body was carried there in a tremendous procession of notables, both foreign and Turkish.

A long circular drive bordered with pines leads up to the mausoleum. We park, and walk up a flight of a hundred stone steps, past a guard of honor, and down a flagstone promenade nearly one eighth of a mile long, flanked by Hittite stone lions. The crypt is open, its roof supported on heavy stone pillars. We join the crowd of Turks moving slowly past the long coffin, with the full-length figure in black of Turkey's national hero, lying on his back. The custom is that persons visiting as a group lay a wreath or flowers at the base of the coffin; other persons just pay their respects. The inner walls of Anit Kabir are carved with statements taken from Ataturk's speeches. There is no other decoration in the building; as one Turk said, "This is not a museum but a national shrine, a place of worship."

It is true; there is a definite element of worship in the behavior of the Turks around us. The public building in America which most nearly parallels the mausoleum, in decoration and use, is the Lincoln Memorial in Washington. In both places profound statements in brief sentences are engraved on the stone walls; in both, the figures of two great men, one lying, one sitting, brood over the visitor. People often leave the Lincoln Memorial with tears in their eyes, they are so deeply moved by Lincoln and all he stands for. The Turks who come and go in the mausoleum are a stolid, disciplined people; there are no sounds in the crypt except the shuffle of feet and heavy breathing. But there is a tremendous electricity in the atmosphere, a feeling of emotion almost overpowering but held back by an effort of will on each person's part. If there is a key to understanding the new Turkey, it is in the mausoleum and the spirit of the man buried there, a man who unified the Turkish past and present—taking the best parts of each—in the three cities of Ankara.

6. City Life

IN MOST OF THE COUNTRIES of the world there is a great difference between the way people live in the city and the way they live in the country. These differences are not so noticeable in our United States, because people everywhere have radio, and television, and automobiles. But don't forget that our country is more advanced materially—we have more gadgets—than any other. The differences in Turkey between city life and country life are extreme. Turkey does not have television. About one out of every 300 Turks owns a car, and that one lives in the city. The average country Turk has little more than a donkey to his name. Turkey's roads are five hundred per cent better than they were thirty years ago; in fact the Turkish industrial network has moved ahead faster in that short time than that of any other nation, even the Soviet Union. Still there is much work to be done. As we drive across the country we will see many, many villages without electricity, many more that are beyond reach of a road. European plumbing is the exception rather than the rule. Life everywhere goes on at a much slower pace than in America. The point is not that the Turks are backward, but that they are different.

Ankara is typical of urban Turkey. Bus travel is perfectly satisfactory (as long as the buses don't break down) to get from one place to another on a fixed itinerary, but not very flexible. You can buy a donkey for 180 Turkish liras, but donkeys break down too, sometimes wilfully. More dependable are taxis or the *dolmuş*—this last a peculiar

Turkish institution. It is a taxi which travels a fixed route, like a bus, but does not leave its starting-point until it has a full load of passengers (dolmuş means full). Most of the dolmuşes in Turkey are vintage Austins or British Fords, held together with baling wire and Scotch tape and the driver's prayers, but they *are* cheap and do seem to hold up.

In addition to the points of interest described in the previous chapter, there are a number of others of more interest to young people. In the Ulus area are the Nineteenth of May Stadium, the Hippodrome, and the Park of Youth. May 19 is Youth Day, which commemorates Ataturk's historic landing at Samsun in 1919 after his "escape" from Istanbul. The stadium was built to honor this event and the young Turkish officers who worked with the Ghazi to make the Republic possible. Each year on that day the stadium is filled to capacity for celebrations and sports events—first a soccer match (the Turks call it football, or *futbol*) between two championship teams, then track and field events, finally mass calisthenics.

Adjoining the stadium is the Ankara Tennis Club, one of two in the city, with a fine modern clubhouse and eight all-weather courts. It is a fine place to play on a summer afternoon under the watchful eyes of storks sitting on their nests in the tops of the poplars.

The Park of Youth, a few blocks away, was built as an act of faith by the Turks who came to Ankara believing the desert could be made green again after centuries of neglect. There is a large artificial lake with a fifty-foot fountain in the park; this lake, with its "border" of poplars, is a landmark both from the air and from the Old City. The Park of Youth also contains an amusement park with a Ferris wheel, and other whirligig rides.

Just off the road to Ayaş and Istanbul in the western part of Ulus is the Hippodrome, a huge open-end arena with an oval trotting track. Occasionally camel fights are held there, but the big day is the Fourth of July, when the American Ambassador treats the entire American community to an Independence Day party. This is the only time of year that American hot dogs, beer, and bottled Coke will be found in bulk on Turkish soil. The Fourth of July party is just like home—games, a midway featuring Turkish belly dancers, camel races, and fireworks. It is exciting to watch the rockets and flower clusters light up the citadel and cliff houses of the Old City in the background—a touch of home in an antique land.

A few miles beyond the Hippodrome, at the railroad station of Ghazi, is the Çiftlik, the experimental farm of Ataturk. It is an old Ankara custom for parents to take their children to Çiftlik for a day's outing; thus the sober Turk mixes his children's pleasure with instruction by example. For Ataturk established the farm to show his people they could grow better things in a barren area by applying the correct principles of irrigation and agriculture. The Çiftlik covers in all one thousand acres; it has more than one hundred thousand trees, poplar, pine, and acacia, a thorny tree which holds water very well in its deep roots. There are enormous fields planted in fruits and vegetables. There is also a model dairy which produces, pasteurizes, and sells both cows' and goats' milk. Ataturk had a summer place on the farm, and spent most of his time driving tractors, milking cows, planting trees.

He encouraged the Turks to come and look at the progress at Çiftlik. As an afterthought he put in a zoo. The farm was given to the nation after his death, and the zoo has become the biggest attraction. There is a train from Ankara to the farm. We get off at Ghazi, and gaily-painted wagons take us to the zoo. It has all the usual birds and animals on display, and plenty of peanuts for elephant and monkey. There are also some odd features, for a zoo. First is the Angora cat, native to the region. There are very few left now. The inbreeding of these cats has produced a very odd cat—blue in one eye, green in the other, and stone-deaf!

The zoo also has a large flock of turkeys—American turkeys, that is. Turkish turkeys, some of which are also kept on display, are smaller and bonier than their American cousins. The third strange exhibit is of dogs. Except for the Anatolian sheep dog the dog is not native to Turkey, and the Turks share the Moslem attitude (descended from

Mohammed) of dislike for the dog as an unclean animal. The sheep dog, being essential, is well-treated, but it is a little unnerving to see cages full of Great Danes, English setters, Pekingese, cocker spaniels, etc., whom the Turks tease unmercifully.

Approximately as far from Ankara as Çiftlik, but to the north instead of the west, is the Çubuk Barrage, another fine excursion spot. It is a dam, and water from the Çubuk River, thus controlled, is piped to Ankara to give the city a permanent water supply, rather important in an area where rain does not fall from April to November except in rare instances. It was near the town of Çubuk that Tamerlane actually won his big battle in 1402 over Beyazit; he then erected the customary tower of skulls. But there is no trace of the tower. We drive to Çubuk through an eroded brown landscape, and come upon the dam suddenly, an irrigated grotto of rich grass, trees, flowers, hidden between dun hills. At Çubuk there is a tiny artificial lake full of ducks, and a pleasant outdoor café beside the water. More than any place in Turkey, the Çubuk Barrage deserves the title "oasis." Minutes after we leave it, it vanishes behind the hills; at the road fork leading back to Ankara the river is a muddy trickle irrigating some spindly peach trees; a mile from town there is no river at all.

Some of the differences between city life in Turkey and what we know at home would be obvious if we were to go shopping. Turkey's variety of climates and soils allows farmers to grow nearly all the fruits and vegetables we know, and some less usual ones, like leeks. Since shopping is a good way to practice one's Turkish and talk to people to get their points of view, suppose we harness up and go to the supermarket. Wait a minute! Where is the supermarket? *Pazar* is a familiar Turkish word for market, but these pazars are tiny places. We discover that we must visit half a dozen shops before we can fill a grocery list. There is the bread man *(ekmekçi)* who sells only bread, in long loaves. Turkish bread is gray, made of unbleached flour, and somewhat tasteless, but it is very good for you.

The pastries we want are not found at the bread shop; for them we must visit a *pastahane*. Here there are many rich desserts like *baklava* (flaky layers of dough soaked in honey), *halva* (almond candy), vizier's finger, and many more.

We will find vegetables and fruit at the market. They are piled on trays in the open, and we look in vain for frozen-food packages. The handsomest Turkish vegetable is eggplant *(patlican)*; all sorts of wonderful dishes like *hunkâr beğendi* ("His Majesty liked it") or *patlican tavasī* (fried) have an eggplant base.

The man in the market weighs everything on a simple scale using small brass weights as balances, and charges us by the kilo (2.2 pounds). He may be willing to bargain over his vegetables, but never over his fruit, for Turkish fruit is a national institution. Each region has its specialty—peaches from Bursa, some over five pounds, pears and apples from Konya and Ankara, figs and raisins from Izmir, grapes from Malatya, huge watermelons from Diyarbakir. When melon rinds begin floating down the Bosphorus, the weather is considered warm enough for swimming. The watermelons we grow are probably descendants of Turkish melons.

Turkish cities have two kinds of butchers. One sells only red meat, beef, lamb, mutton, rarely veal. Pork is neither sold nor eaten by Turks, as it is prohibited under the Moslem religion. The poultry butcher sells poultry and odd things like rabbits, in season. Fish rarely appears in inland Anatolian markets, and when it comes in it must be bought right away, as there is no refrigeration.

Turkish meat is undeniably tough, but restaurant chefs do great things with it. The best (and safest) meat in both back-country *lokantas* and smart city places like Abdullah's in Istanbul and Karpiç's in Ankara, is *şiş kebab*, pieces of lamb broiled on a skewer alternating with onion and green pepper. If you have the time, another specialty is *döner kebab*, lamb sides broiled on a big vertical spit and sliced thin. Circassian chicken was a favorite of Ataturk's—the secret is in the sauce. *Boereks*, for lunch, are cylinders of dough filled with chopped meat. The best Turkish cooking is done on a *mangal* (charcoal grill);

the best way to discover Turkish cuisine is to go into the kitchen and choose your dinner.

An important element in Turkish economic life is provided by the various salesmen, or rather pedlars, who drift around the cities offering services, buying and selling. For example, in every major Turkish city neighborhood, at some time during the day, will be heard a strange cry, "Eskee-jee." The *eskici*—he calls his name—buys old clothes, which he then sells to second-hand clothing stores to be resold to customers. The increasing numbers of Europeans and Americans resident in Turkey make the eskici a useful middleman, and many enterprising eskicis have branched out into the used furniture and appliance business; some grapevine tells them when a family is about to return to the States, and they appear at its door in droves.

One of the real tragedies of Turkey's inflation after 1954 has been the disappearance of coffee. The world's first "coffee break" came in Istanbul in 1554 when some unknown Ottoman bureaucrat discovered he could work better after a pause for a cup of coffee, and since then the thick, bitter Turkish brew has been a staple of the office-worker. It used to accompany all dinners, all official visits; after a heavy dinner a demitasse of Turkish coffee, either *sade* (without sugar), *orta* (a little) or *çok* (a lot) of sugar really settled the stomach. During the day boys were employed regularly by offices as "coffee runners" and sent to the coffeehouses by their employers to carry back coffee in cups on small long-handled brass trays, a custom as pleasant then and as absent now as the five-cent subway ride.

In general Turks drink less hard liquor than Westerners; it is a matter of habit with them rather than the general Moslem prohibition on alcohol. The national drink is *raki,* which is made from raisins and flavored with anise and tastes like licorice. No one should be fooled by its clear, harmless appearance in a glass. Pour some water in the raki, and it will turn milky. "Afiyet olsun!" is the proper toast; then you down the raki at a gulp, in the Swedish fashion. Many formal dinners begin with raki and hors d'oeuvres, and no one should be foolish enough to drink it without eating at the same time.

Another Turkish beverage (and custom) is *ayran*, a type of buttermilk. On a hot summer day ayran is better and cooler than lemonade; in some mountain villages the peasants greet the villager with a bowl of ayran. Related to ayran is *yoğurt*, which is sold in little crocks, and made from sour cream. The yoğurt you buy in stores like the *bakkal* (a sort of dry grocer who sells staples like chick-peas, flour, olive oil) looks awful, as it has a thick gray crust. But break through that crust, and you will find a delicious cold dessert, extremely digestible. Turkish babies are frequently weaned on yoğurt. And hospitals prescribe it for certain diets.

Turkey produces her own wine and beer, the best wine being from the Kavaklidere and Çankaya sections of Ankara. She also imports (and phoneticizes) *skoç viski* and *votka,* and produces her own *likorus, kanyak, krem di ment,* and *vermut.* You will sometimes find dairies which produce and sell cows' milk; this is pasteurized but the bottles are not. Rather than the cow, the goat is milked regularly, and one of the national delicacies is white goat cheese.

As more and more visitors reach this land that was so isolated culturally under the Ottomans, more familiar forms of Western entertainment develop. The State Opera in Ankara, for example, does all the familiar operas, in Turkish. One can stay at home to see opera, of course, but a type of entertainment peculiar to the Turks, and one worth coming thousands of miles to see, is the Karagöz, a very old folk drama native to Anatolia. It is actually a puppet show for small children, but grownups usually laugh harder at performances than their offspring do. Karagöz (Black Eyes), his friend Hacīvad, and the other characters are puppets. Dressed in sixteenth century Ottoman village costumes, they put on shadow plays behind a lighted screen, accompanied by traditional music on the *saz* (a kind of violin), a bass viol, and a *davul* (drum). The Karagöz stories were a sort of reaction by the villagers to the oppression of their Ottoman governors; the little

puppets were able to satirize authorities and poke fun at human weaknesses without being punished, and through them the villagers let off
steam, could even laugh at their hard existence.

One other element in Turkish life which you have probably heard
of is the *hammam,* or Turkish bath. Turkey is not well supplied with
bathtubs or showers, and the hammam is essential to national cleanli-
ness. Hammams in some cities, like Bursa, are beautiful buildings;
others are simple square buildings, with separate wings for men and
women. You enter your particular wing, shuck off your clothes, and
join a group soaping vigorously under hot water. Then you lie flat on
a stone table and are scrubbed with a coarse glove by attendants who
really know their trade, and remove a pound or so of skin from what
you thought was a clean body. Don't be surprised, it always happens.
Then comes a siesta in a steam room, and finally you dress and depart,
feeling unbelievably clean and ready for anything—even a dusty drive
into the heart of Anatolia.

7. Meet the People

"Turks are in general husky, tall, robust people with tough but noble faces. Under their black eyebrows sparkle their clever eyes. . . . The Turk speaks with restraint; he will not open his mouth before first thinking. . . . Turks love music, flowers, perfumes, sweets, and coffee. The Turk's kindness and generosity is even extended to animals; they would stop anybody attempting to kill an animal and would ask him in anger, 'Can you create such a life?'"
(from *Byzantino Turcica*, by Skarlatos Vizantios)

B Y NOW we have some definite ideas about the Turk— what he eats and drinks, how he spends his leisure hours, and how modern Turkey came into existence. We are about ready to put together a composite portrait of Turkish characteristics. Why not base it on the above quotation? It certainly describes the Turks—but it was written in 1852. Or perhaps we can read a few magazine articles about the Turks; how they are America's best friend in the Middle East, our democratic, loyal ally, very brave, quick to understand modern industrial technology. Between these two we ought to have a clear picture of the Turk, since fundamental attitudes do not change much in a hundred years, and Vizantios' picture should still be true.

Unfortunately the quotation is a superficial view, making the same mistake that many article writers do, of failing to note that Turks are a different people. We must judge them by their Turkishness, not their Americanness or Britishness. Some of the qualities that make up a Turk are good, some bad. People like the Hungarians and Bulgarians, who were conquered by the Turks, called them "The Unspeakable Turks." The British, who have always gotten on well with the Turks, call them "The Englishmen of the Orient." The Arabs, also subject peoples for centuries, have another opinion. It all depends on one's point of view, based on experience.

The city crowds we see strolling along Ataturk Boulevard, taking the sea air on the Karsīyaka at Izmir, or crossing the Galata Bridge in Istanbul, look familiar at first. The men wear European suits, the women, print dresses or skirts and heavy wool sweaters. Many men wear felt caps. They do not appear to be in such a hurry as a New York crowd, and they are quieter, perhaps more disciplined. Except for these minor differences, and the different language—though we will often hear French and English spoken along with Turkish—we could be in one of the big cities at home. Ankara, particularly, looks like any Western capital.

When we take a closer look, however, we find qualities which set the Turk apart from all other people and clearly identify him. We find a great variety in physical type, as we would expect from the many different peoples who left their mark on Anatolia. There are blue-eyed blond Turks in the crowd—one village near Lake Van in eastern Anatolia is populated entirely with these, descended from Norman knights. There are fair-skinned Circassians, originally from the Caucasus; Circassian women were so famous for their beauty and perfect measurements that the Sultans imported them in droves for the royal harems. There are red-haired Turks, possibly from North Europe or Germany. We see Mongolian types, Turkomans with narrow eyes and high cheekbones, Greeks with olive complexions, occasionally even a Hittite face with its huge hooked nose. Yet this thoroughly mixed-up crowd considers itself *Turkish*, nothing else. Once I asked a boy in an Aegean village if his parents had been Greek. He told me no, they were all Turks. Yet he was the classic Greek physical type, curly black hair, jet eyes, feminine in physique rather than hard and muscular.

There is a dominant Turkish type in this diversity, however. The men are short, averaging about five feet six inches, and stocky, with black or dark-brown hair and handsome dark eyes. Turkish girls are usually plump, with long black hair worn in chignons or pigtails and beautiful almond eyes. Many are extremely beautiful, and Turkey's Miss Universe entrant often places high in the international beauty contest. The plumpness of the girls is "by request." One girl, a member of a prominent family and married to an engineer, did not follow the pattern and remained slender, although her face and figure were extraordinary. Both her family and her husband's worried over her constantly. They came to her house every day solemnly bringing trays of pastries "to fatten Nevin."

Turks have a special *look,* also, which makes them Turks and not Englishmen or Americans or Bantus. They are pale, sober, unsmiling, and wear a poker face in public. Yet their look is candid, direct, quizzical, the look of a people serious about their responsibilities.

The Turkish characteristic which you will undoubtedly meet first and most often is hospitality. Even though they cannot offer any more than little cups of Turkish coffee, their hospitality is tremendous. Every visitor comes away with half a dozen stories of this open-handed welcome. Ours comes about through a visit to Etlik, a village on the rim of one of the hills that girdle Ankara. From Ulus Square we climb swiftly and steeply past pink villas hidden behind orchards heavy with fruit. At the crest of one ridge we stop at a rambling yellow stucco house. We are introduced to the Turkish family living there, a man and his wife and two grown sons, plus assorted small fry. "Hoş geldiniz! (Welcome!)" they say. "Hoş bulduk! (We have found pleasure!)" we reply. We are given chairs, while the family stands around us shyly answering questions. The wife disappears inside the house, and in jig time trays of pastries, bowls of fruit, tea steaming in small tapered glasses, all materialize from the unseen kitchen. The hospitality is so natural and swift that we hardly realize we are unexpected guests and have given the hostess no warning at all.

The father presses us to try the fruit. "We grow it all here," he says. "We have several acres." He shows his land, crowded with apple, pear, almond and peach trees, grapevines, and a melon patch. He and his sons are perfect examples of the "terrible Turk" we have heard about, strongly built with fierce cruel eyes and sweeping mustaches. They are also perfect gentlemen. We learn by accident we are sitting on the only chairs in the house—a house without bath rooms, refrigeration, heat, or running water. No family at home (and this Turkish family has an annual income of a few hundred dollars) could approximate the hospitality we find at Etlik. The short visit lengthens into hours, until the fruit bowls are almost empty and the lights of Ankara begin to twinkle below, spread out like a jeweled carpet.

A Turkish characteristic which is related to hospitality is an extraordinary interest in Americans. The most popular buildings in Turkish cities are the American libraries sponsored by the U.S. Information Agency, because there Turks can read about America. The interest is so great that in Edirne, for example, where there was no library, a Turk who had learned English set up his own Turkish-American Cultural Association, started conversational classes, and a library of American books to boot. Young people from the United States can expect to be asked all sorts of questions, some of them extremely personal, by young Turks. You should certainly not be insulted if a Turkish boy or girl asks you, on first acquaintance, if you are married, if you are rich, and even what kind of underwear you wear. These questions are the Turkish way of satisfying a great curiosity about us.

The family is the basic unit in Turkish society, and Turks are great family men. The men tend to spend many hours at the coffeehouses with other men, but the off-duty pleasures are usually shared with the family. The commonest pleasure is a family walk on "main street," at a leisurely pace to allow *Anné* (Mother) and the girls to window-shop, while *Baba* (Father) and his son stroll hand in hand and discuss more important things. Frequently the son is also attracted to window displays, and Baba strolls on, hands knotted behind his back, until the family catches up. His special pride is his son, although he loves all his daughters nearly as much; it is a secretly unhappy Turk who does not have at least one son, preferably the oldest child.

The closeness of family relationships even extends to the relatives, and Turkish families have an uncommonly large number of relatives. When groups of relatives meet on such a stroll, the men kiss on both cheeks in the French manner, and the women follow suit. Then the children, who have been hanging back shyly, are brought forward. Each child places his forehead on the backs of his uncle's hands (or aunt's, or grandmother's, or grandfather's), as a sort of blessing, and then kisses the hands lightly. Then everyone begins to chatter in the universal fashion of relatives who don't see each other often enough.

Turks have a number of customs which may seem odd to us. For instance, in big towns and small cities such as Adapazari or Bolu, where the unpaved main street doubles as the national highway, the Turks stroll down the middle of the street. The street is also used for various purposes by dogs, oxcarts, donkeys, bullock-teams, and miscellaneous herds of cattle, sheep, and goats. An American car trying to get through town finds itself in a monumental traffic jam, caused not by the animal population but by the people. They are still so unused to cars that even a horn doesn't move them, and when a car does thread its way through the foot traffic it may well find a Turk or two draped over the front fender.

Many Turks, like our Etlik friends, also wear pajamas all day at home. They are very fond of loud striped ones, and I've known respectable Turkish businessmen to answer the door in these. The custom has various explanations—to cut down on laundry bills, save on the good Sunday suit—but probably pajamas are a popular compromise between European dress and the outlawed, but comfortable baggy trousers of the Empire.

Another curious custom, to us, is to see two grown men walking down the street holding hands. For some reason soldiers do this more than civilians. Whatever the reason, you are advised not to tease a couple of burly Turkish infantrymen about it.

A Turkish habit which often baffles the unwary is built around the word *Yok,* which means "there isn't any," but is used as a colloquial

"No." Let's say you want to buy some Kütahya pottery (a glazed ware decorated with green and blue designs) to send home to Aunt Mary. You find a store which looks as if it might carry this pottery in stock. You walk in, and ask the proprietor in your best kitchen Turkish if he has this pottery. He doesn't answer. Instead he lifts his chin and rolls his eyes toward heaven, purses his lips, and makes a slight clicking noise with his teeth. Don't be fooled, as one lady tourist was, into asking the same question several times and going away with the firm conviction that all Turks are instinctively rude. This gesture is a form of shorthand that saves the shopkeeper from repeating again and again, "Yok, effendim, we don't carry that."

Turks are hospitable, independent-minded, reserved and unemotional in public (except when greeting relatives and close friends). Turkish honesty toward visitors is outstanding in the Middle East. There are many examples of this—the hamal who carried our luggage to the ferry in Istanbul, the hall porter in a hotel who refused a tip because he thought he was paid enough for his work, the complete safety of one's belongings while traveling.

Normally Turks are docile and well-disciplined; they obey laws and are not very demonstrative. The discipline of the Turkish forces in Korea, even when captured, was proverbial. Captured Turks maintained their own military organization, and took orders from their own officers instead of their Chinese captors. Another characteristic of Turks is the number of surprising superstitions they have. Even well-educated Turks, for example, may believe that people go mad during the full moon. They say a blue bead protects a new baby from the evil eye. Every truck and bus, also, has *Maşallah* (What God hath wrought!) painted on it, usually above the windshield, to ward off the same evil eye.

It's a common assumption that in the Orient you must bargain for everything you buy, and if you are dealing with a Greek, Arab, or Armenian merchant you can usually expect him to set a higher price for something than you intend to pay for it. These merchants consider haggling as part of the game of life, to be carried on over innumerable cups of coffee. The more interest you show in an article, the more you must pay for it, but *never* the asking price. But bargaining is not as common in Turkey as in other parts of Asia. The Turks were administrators and soldiers, but they scorned commerce, and left this profession in the hands of conquered races like the Greeks and Arabs. Bargaining does exist, particularly in such places as the Grand Bazaar in Istanbul, which derives most of its trade from tourists. If you want to take home one of the wonderfully thick, soft Turkish carpets (and who doesn't?), and invite one of the traveling carpet salesmen to your house or hotel room, you can expect considerable haggling.

In general, Anatolia is not an artistic region, for the departure of the Greeks and Armenians after the Turkish Republic exchanged populations in 1922 robbed Turkey of most of its artisans. There are few handicrafts to be bought today except antiques, and these are often Iranian or Arab. Turkish carpets are justly famed; next in artistic interest are copper and brass trays and dishes. Copper utensils, being useful as well as interesting, are turned out by the thousands. The coppersmiths' guild operates along an entire street in the Old City of Ankara, for example; the process is to buy a copper tray or dish from one shop, then take it to another to have it tinplated for permanent value. We might expect to have to bargain on the "Street of Copper," and often do. But it depends on the mood of the seller. If he thinks our price is too low, he will refuse to sell at all and close his shop, considering our offer an insult to his pride.

Turkish arrogance and cruelty are qualities which you may never meet. Unfortunately they do exist. When he was striving to build Turkey's national morale, Ataturk sent a famous poet around Anatolia to teach the people to say, like a catechism, "I am a Turk: my race and language are great." Inevitably the repetition of this saying gave the Turks an aggressive feeling of superiority. Some of the acts you may encounter—the refusal of merchants to sell, the pushiness of Turkish crowds, the rare flashes of dislike of foreigners (in September,

1955, the long-dormant anger of Turks at Greeks exploded in destructive riots)—are really a kind of compensation for the centuries when the Ottoman Empire was a punching bag for the big powers of Europe.

Turkish arrogance is also shown in the common sensitivity to criticism. A teacher is immune to this sensitivity, because the teacher is always right. But criticize Turkish officials on their policy, or a Turkish mechanic for poor maintenance, and they turn prickly-resentful. The Turk is convinced he can do everything better than anyone else, and this self-confidence gets him into difficult spots.

These are some of the less desirable features of the Turkish character. They are heavily outweighed by the good characteristics. Even though he is prickly about foreign criticism, the Turk can laugh at himself realistically. From his national funnyman, Nasrettin Hoca, he has inherited a love of puncturing inflated personalities. A popular Hoca story goes like this: Once Hoca was invited to a wedding. He arrived late after a long journey, with no time to change from his work clothes. Nobody paid him any attention. Later Hoca was invited to another wedding. This time he wore a fine sable coat and a good suit. He was asked to the head of the table for the wedding feast. As the plates were passed, Hoca held out a corner of his coat to his plate and said, "Eat, my fur coat! All these honors are for you!"

The genuine interest in Americans, the hospitality, and the generosity of the Turkish people are what you will remember from your Turkish holiday. Their pleasures are less complicated than ours, and conducted at a much slower pace. When the sultans were in control of Turkey, it was very difficult for boys and girls to meet except in secret, dating was unknown, and marriages were arranged by the parents. A lad who became interested in a harem girl in Constantinople, for example, developed an elaborate code based on flowers to make dates with his love. He would have been beheaded, at best, if caught, but he was not, and his "language of flowers" survives in the corsage and birthday roses. Young people usually knew something about each other from the reports of intermediaries, before they were engaged, but they never had any time to be together before marriage. That is all changed now, and boys and girls meet at dances, go to movies together, get acquainted at the *lycée* or university. The lycée (*lisé,* in Turkish) is their equivalent of our high school, except that it covers six grades instead of the usual four. Turkish boys and girls who graduate from lycée have really had two years of college, and passed some very tough examinations, so that they are more mature than most of our high-school seniors. By the time a Turkish boy is ready to marry he has a pretty good idea of the sort of girl he wants. Even so, he will not often go against the wishes of his parents.

This continued, ingrained parental respect and the closeness of the family unit, explains why the Turks set so much store by their holidays *(bayrams).* The longest and most important of these is *Şeker Bayram,* a chapter in itself. Next comes *Kurban Bayram* (Festival of Sacrifices), which commemorates Abraham's attempted sacrifice of his son Isaac after God had tested him by ordering him to do so (Genesis, xxii). Just as Abraham did, the Turks sacrifice a sheep on this Moslem holy day. For weeks beforehand we will see flocks of sheep, their backs splashed with orange paint, being driven into town for the sacrifice ritual. On the day of *Kurban Bayram* each family that can afford it rises early, dresses in their best clothes, makes the sacrifice, gives the meat of the sheep to the poor, and spends the day visiting. All this is done as a family, never alone.

One other holiday, *Çocuk Bayram* (Children's Festival) is another clue to Turkish character. On the twenty-third of April all schools are closed, and the young children march. The boys wear uniforms of black tunics and knickers, the girls black smocks over white dresses, their hair in pigtails bound with huge white bows. The pride and happiness of Turkish parents watching their children marching along are unforgettable.

8. The Village and the Villager

DO YOU REMEMBER our journey to Hattusas, the ancient Hittite capital? Along the gravel highway from Ankara, we might have noticed a number of small arrow-shaped signs. (Similar signs are found on all of Turkey's new roads). They are about a foot long and six inches wide, made of wood, with letters scrawled on them in whitewash. The letters are hard to read, and why would anyone notice or stop to read a tiny sign that points to nowhere, away from the road, when traveling at forty miles an hour? All these signs would say would be "3 km. to such-and-such *köy*." It wouldn't mean a thing to us.

To Turks those small signs mean a great deal. They mean that home is about two miles away over the hill. *Köy* means village, and four out of every five Turks are *köylus,* or villagers. They are quite different from their city cousins. City Turks, even if born in villages, become angry when they speak of the "backwardness" of the villagers. But the villagers cannot be blamed for being less advanced than the city dwellers. They had almost no contact with the outside world after the fifteenth century, when the old caravan trade was replaced by sea trade with the discoveries of Columbus and Vasco da Gama. Most Turkish villagers never heard of modern machinery or doctors or education or world wars until the road came to them in the 1950's. Now more and more of them do, and they are really taking part in national life, voting and discussing politics.

Boğazköy, below Hattusas, is itself a köy. Because foreign archaeologists came there to dig, the village learned about the new world earlier than most Turkish villages. In fact, in 1931 those workers hired to help an archaeological expedition went on strike, protesting the requirement that the local manor lord receive a cut from their wages. They didn't think it was right in a republic.

In 1950 this new preoccupation of the peasants with national affairs produced startling results. The people of Boğazköy voted in Turkey's first free, secret national elections, along with their fellow köylus and urbanite Turks, and turned Ataturk's party out of office. They made Adnan Menderes, a farmer's son though of a rich land-owning family, Prime Minister. In two subsequent elections, 1954 and 1957, the villagers voted to continue the new democratic experiment, in the latter case despite inflation and no coffee. This stunning overthrow of the party of modern Turkey's founder, cannot be explained unless it is studied through the eyes of the villager. The Anatolian has a proverb: "You have a horseshoe; if you find three more horseshoes and a donkey, you can ride your donkey." It helps to explain the election of 1950, which was not at all phenomenal, merely a case of the villager finding a donkey to ride and three more horseshoes.

The village of Balgat, east of Bahçelievler and south of the Military Academy, is a good showcase of the life of the köylu since 1950. Before then Balgat could have been half an hour by car from the capital, *if* it had had a road. But it had no road, and lay forgotten, its crumbling mud-brick hovels clinging to a hillside, practically under the noses of the educated Turks who fought so hard to modernize their country. Since time immemorial Balgat was run by a *muhtar,* or headman. Being muhtar meant having the best land, and the power to issue and collect ration cards, collect taxes, arbitrate civil disputes. Before 1950 the muhtar of Balgat had the only radio in the village. The evening entertainment of Balgatis was to sit around the muhtar's house and listen to the news from Ankara. At the end of each broadcast the muhtar explained and analyzed the news for his associates. This enter-

tainment, naturally, was for the men of the village. Although the
women worked in the fields alongside their husbands and brothers,
their place after dark was at home.

Today the world has caught up with Balgat—or vice versa. The
village is half an hour from Ankara by road. A daily bus service takes
the köylu every hour on the hour to Ulus Station. For a few kuruş he
can commute to his job like any American or see the bright lights of
the city. Most of the farmers of Balgat are commuters now, and rent
their farmland to less ambitious (or perhaps wiser) villagers. More
than a hundred of Balgat's rooftops are decorated with radio antennas,
and the women of the village listen as solemnly as the men. The muhtar
himself is out of a job; Balgat has been incorporated into greater
Ankara. The blessings of civilization have reached this köy; electricity,
a stable water supply, a traffic cop. There is no question of Balgat's
support for the new ways. Balgat's main concern, in fact, is how to
keep boys from asking girls for dates on the edge of town instead of
going through the usual parental channels.

Not all Turkish villages are as fortunate as Balgat. As you travel
about Anatolia, you will see many of them, silhouetted on ridges, which
have no road, no arrow-shaped sign even. Their squat outlines make
them seem part of the ridge, and indeed they are part of the land, the
"villages that time forgot." The earnest young schoolteacher assigned
to start a school in such a village must travel many days on a donkey
or by foot to get there. When he arrives, he will find köylus still plow-
ing their land with a wood needle plow drawn by oxen (if the köylu
is rich enough to have oxen). The men will still be wearing *shalvars*,
the bell-bottomed Ottoman trousers; the women, veils and pajama-type
bloomers in preference to skirts. He will find total illiteracy, a high
rate of disease, a desperately low standard of living—and he may find
ignorance, superstition, the mental outlook of the Middle Ages. Such
a schoolteacher was Mahmut Makal, who went to a village in a very
poor section of Anatolia near Tuz Gölü (Salt Lake), and wrote a book
about his experiences which was so shocking in its revelations that for

a time he was imprisoned as a Communist. The authorities believed that such things could not possibly be true, and therefore Makal was trying to undermine the Government!

But such villages are an ever-shrinking minority, and in fact Western-educated Turks feel much more strongly about the backwardness of their villagers than we, who would probably mourn the disappearance of picturesque customs. The typical köy is in a state of transition, and the typical köylu feels that as progress continues the old Turkish ways, of honesty, courage, steadiness and discipline will come forward to strengthen the nation.

Here is a typical köy named Yavruçuk, not far from Ankara near some Hittite carvings. Unless you were looking for these carvings you would go right through the village without stopping. You probably would not even notice it, for one characteristic of this village, like others on the plateau which have no natural protection like an escarpment, is that it has relied on unobtrusiveness in the past to escape the attention of raiding parties. Its mud-brick houses are huddled together in a small dip in the ground, around a stream. It has no Sokoni Vakum gas station, no accommodations, no factories, no medical center. There are two public buildings, a coffeehouse and a sort of machine shop where parts for an old tractor and miscellaneous rusted machinery are kept by the local wheat pool. The village is raked by fierce storms in winter and beaten by the sun in summer. The only building materials are mud-brick and dung, and the latter is so precious, being used for roofing, heat, and cooking, that toward the end of the winter a man with a good dung pile is practically a millionaire. What little wood the people of Yavruçuk have comes from cutting off the tops of the willow trees that line the banks of their stream; this is unsound forestry which gives the trees the look of men with stiff green heads.

Village life is undeniably hard. The women must wash without soap in the cold stream, beating clothes against flat stones. Men rise at dawn, the shepherds going off with their flocks, the farmers to the fields of wheat which Yavruçuk owns. The workday is from dawn to dusk. Village women seem to work even harder than men, for in addition to their household duties we see them in the fields, while the men foregather in the coffeehouse every morning. This is not an idle time, however; marriages are contracted, land bought and sold, politics discussed, over cups of hot tea. The arrival of visitors like ourselves is the signal for the traditional Anatolian courtesy. "Buyrun!" the men say, meaning "Welcome!" We are invited in, and offered the center table. Tea arrives, elaborate expressions of courtesy exchanged, before the nature of the visit is established and the necessary business, finding a guide to the carvings, settled. Instead of sitting, the men form a ring around us. They wear second-hand suits, undoubtedly acquired by an eskici, felt caps, heavy boots over thick woollen socks—their costume both winter and summer. They look rough and fierce, but are instinctively polite, with manners that come from the heart and absolute honesty. It is impossible for us to pay for tea, in Yavruçuk or any other köy, though the change in our pockets might equal a year's wages for some of the men.

The great event in the life of this village, under the new government, is not the arrival of foreign visitors, but of a school. The schoolmaster, himself trained in a Village Institute, which teaches villagers to teach other villagers both to read and to farm more profitably, has come to occupy a position second to the muhtar and even to replace that traditional magistrate. Everyone in the village goes to school, boys and girls by day, old men at night, where they learn their letters by the light of a sheep's-fat candle.

The Hittite carvings, called Gavur Kalesi (Infidel Castle) are three miles from the village, over a cart road. They are interesting—two gigantic figures carved on the vertical face of a cliff—but not as interesting as the shepherd who materializes—no other word will do—from behind a boulder. He is typical, a powerfully built man, his face deeply lined, wearing the hide of a sheep turned inside out and moccasins to match. He carries a flute, and upon request begins to play. Suddenly the silence of Anatolia is filled with melody, a sad, incredibly haunting tune that echoes all the tragic history of this land.

In spite of their poverty and their hard lives, most of the villagers refuse to move away, or go to the city to find work. Their attitude is expressed by one who says he did, but that he "couldn't breathe there; too many smells," and returned.

There are two other types of villages in Turkey. One is the escarpment type, a village whose houses have been dug into the side of a cliff. One escarpment village, curiously enough, is in the heart of Ankara; it is the Old City. Escarpment villages are vanishing as villagers move down to the river valleys or to more fertile regions. The need for protection from hostile invasion is not vital any more, while the need for better agriculture still is.

The other type is found in these river valleys. Anatolia's rivers, like the Kizil Irmak, the Sakarya, and the Büyük Menderes (from it we get our word "meander" because it does just that), are not navigable; they are broad and fairly shallow. Because of them the river-valley villagers grow a great variety of crops, even cotton, and in contrast to the somber outlines of the plateau, the valley is alive with color.

Suppose we take a look at the valley of the Kizil Irmak (Red River), a river the color of dried blood. We see much wildlife: flocks of field-fares, small black birds with white outer tail feathers; the hoopoe (called the convict bird because of his striped black-and-white back), with his orange breast, his crest and fan-shaped tail; magpies scolding from every poplar, and tall storks strolling beside the water. Small animals like gophers, called *tarla faresi*, dart across the furrows.

The human element is as colorful as the animal: shepherds with their huge sheep dogs, women in printed bloomers and gay *yazmas* (kerchiefs) scattering seeds, men riding donkeys, jitney buses piled high with suitcases and packed with country people on holiday. A farm family passes slowly in a cart drawn by two black oxen; the farmer drives, with his wife, shrouded in black, beside him, and miscellaneous

children, grandparents, chickens, and furniture behind. Moving day
in Anatolia!

Kalecik, in the Kizil Irmak valley, is a typical river-valley köy. Its
entrance is marked by a stone bridge guarded by two stone Roman
lions; this bridge crosses a dry stream bed which is flooded several
hundred yards wide in the rainy season. The köylu of Kalecik has a
curious attitude toward these lions, and for that matter toward his
peninsula's long history. If you ask him who first built the bridge, and
the lions, he will say that they are very old *Turkish!* Similarly the people of Selimiye (ancient Side) on the southern coast build their house
walls of broken Greek columns, Roman statues, old pottery, indifferent
to the value of these remains. They care only about finding construction materials. The people of Kalecik are as indifferent to the Byzantine castle that sits on a hill behind their houses, as to these lions.

Kalecik is a richer köy than Yavruçuk; most river-valley villages are
better off than their plateau or escarpment counterparts. Its mud-brick
houses have thatched roofs, some even window glass. The best families
have two-story houses with wooden porches upstairs, where bunches
of red peppers hang drying. There are no paved sidewalks or streets,
but there is electricity. Some consumers are so proud of their electric
bulbs that they leave them on, swinging from a cord on the ceiling, all
night. On Kalecik's main square are *two* coffeehouses, a *lokanta* (for
strangers, as Kalecik eats at home), a bakkal, a handsome three-story
building with a red tile roof (the *belediye,* or municipal headquarters),
and a statue of Ataturk, next to the mosque (which is full on Fridays
at prayer).

You may be fortunate enough to see some of Anatolia's vanishing
folk customs, by being in a village at the right time. One of these is the
dancing bear. Trained bears from the Caucasus still wander with their
trainer from village to village, away from the main roads. Once they
carried letters, public announcements, songs and stories, from one isolated place to another. Now they are merely wanderers; however, the
arrival of a dancing bear in a village still means a local holiday. Every-

one in town, young and old, crowds around to watch the bear do his act. First he does a jig, stamping in time to the beat of a tambourine. Then he rolls in the dust, shakes hands all around, dances some more, and then makes his trainer dance while *he* beats time. The crowd loves it. When the bear passes the tambourine, turned bottom up as a collection plate, even the poorest köylu can find a few kurus in his pocket.

Perhaps you can time your village visit to coincide with one of the traditional feasts, like the feast of circumcision, or the *pilav zerde,* the Anatolian wedding. Pilav, or rice, is a staple of Turkish diet, and the wedding gets its name from the rice-and-saffron pudding served at the marriage feast. This type of wedding, which only the wealthier villagers can afford, goes on for several days. European clothes are replaced by the old costumes, dresses of heavy brocade, bell-bottomed shalvars, stiff silk headdresses and veils. Old Turkish dances, like the zeybek, given by two groups of men who wheel and stamp their feet, whirling like Cossacks with drawn knives in their hands, are still seen on special occasions like bayrams.

The most important folk festival which survives in Anatolia (now that the Karagöz has gone to the city) is greased wrestling. Wrestling, even above futbol, is Turkey's national sport. The national championships are held each year around St. George's Day (May 6) at Kırkpınar in Thrace, near Edirne. No one knows why a Christian saint should be so honored by a Turkish Muslim festival, but Sultan Murad I, in 1360, first started the event which determines the best *pehlivan* in Turkey. The contestants coat their bodies with olive oil, then wrestle to music from a *zurna,* a kind of oboe, and drum, until one pins the other flat on his back. Formerly they wrestled to the death, but this proved to be rather hard on manpower, so now the wrestling is for a fall. For a year the champion is the most important man in the country, next to the President and Prime Minister.

As the villagers become more and more road-conscious, and their horizons widen, these traditional activities will probably disappear. There is little folk art in Turkey anyway, and city people are in a hurry to have the country people look and act as they do. Turks are too individualistic ever to be cut from exactly the same round of cheese, however, and there is something reassuring about an Anatolian villager riding a donkey loaded on each side with a deep wicker basket full of jars of olive oil. The donkey may be slow and balky and stubborn, but so is his master, and a lot more patient. Eventually both will reach their destination.

9. Sentimental Journeys

"Four or five days journey?" (from Ilghaz to Ankara),
Feride said. "But how vast this Anatolia is!"
"Yes, it is rather large," Hassan agreed.
(*The Dark Moment,* by Ann Bridge)

TODAY A MODERN MOTORCAR can cover the distance from the pine forests of Ilghaz to the capital of new Turkey in about four hours, more than twenty times as fast as a horse-drawn carriage could manage on a rutted track in 1920. But this telescoping of distance has not really reduced the vastness of Anatolia. The rugged terrain also discourages travel. A perfectly ordinary fishing trip to a recommended spot on the Sakarya River, for example, takes all day and into the night, and requires you to traverse first a paved road, next a gravel road, then a jeep track; the last five miles are overland through the fields. The distances encourage mirages, although Anatolia is steppe country, not desert. The typical mirage is a line of poplars marking a river, apparently quite close, which retreats but never seems to leave the horizon.

Inland Turkey is not yet geared to tourism; hotels are sparse and lacking amenities, good restaurants almost nonexistent. Don't let this affect you; it is all too easy to criticize the Turks for what they have not done, instead of praising them for their accomplishments over a relatively short time. Barely a handful of Americans went to Turkey before World War II; even Europeans regarded the country as a place of exile rather than a vacation attraction. The persons best prepared for traveling there, and who seem to have the most fun, are cyclists who carry their gear on their backs.

There are four more or less distinct regions in Turkey to see. In the northwest is Istanbul, a spectacle by itself; but no one in his right mind would stop with Istanbul when nearby are beaches, ski resorts, and the incomparable old Ottoman capital Bursa. In western Turkey is the Izmir region, full of ancient Greek cities like Pergamum, Ephesus, and Sardis, impressive even in ruins. The south has the wild Taurus Mountain range, and the narrow subtropical belt called the Turkish Riviera. Within easy reach of Ankara are alpine lakes, volcanic mountains, and medieval fortified cities spread over central Anatolia.

A few well-chosen words of advice ought to simplify your journeyings about Turkey. It is definitely pioneering away from the big cities. Discount reports of bedbugs and other vermin; hotel rooms are antiseptically clean, and country restaurant food usually is cooked in enough olive oil to purify it. Many establishments have no "European" plumbing. Anatolian food, away from metropolitan centers, is tasteless and without variety; there are no charming country inns as yet. Travel by any means is rugged. The excellent DHY (Turkish State Airways) touches the big cities, but from there on one must resort to taxis, hired car, or trust a bus-driver and his *maşallah*. The main thing to remember is, relax. Then you can enjoy the richly varied scenery, the ruins, the genuine hospitality and friendliness of the citizenry.

"Down East" from Ankara, is Kayseri, a dusty city with a big cotton textile factory. The people of Kayseri have a reputation for sharpness, thus the Turkish proverb: "He can't read or write, but he comes from Kayseri." Added to this is the story of the Kayseri man who sold his white donkey to a buyer. Later, seeing the donkey tied nearby, he stole it back, painted it black, and resold it to the same buyer.

The most interesting of an odd lot of monuments in Kayseri is the Döner Kumbet, or "Turning Mausoleum." It is shaped like a cone, built of blocks of reddish sandstone, with a "chimney-pot" full of straw at the top. The arches at the base are blind, that is, filled in so they lead nowhere, and this gives the mausoleum the illusion of continually turning. Like the Taj Mahal, it was built in memory of a Moslem princess.

West of Kayseri, in the valley of Göreme and adjacent valleys, is Turkey's strangest attraction, the rock cones of Cappadocia. Two huge mountains, Erciyas Dağ (12,848 feet) and Hasan Dağ (10,673 feet) dominate the plain, and are responsible for a formation so weird that when Paul Lucas, in his *Voyage au Levant* (1705) described it, no one believed him, and he was called in France "the useless tourist." Both mountains are extinct volcanoes; ages ago each literally poured rivers of hot lava over the native limestone of the region. The lava fused with the limestone, and as the mass grew cool, it cracked, making what we call tuff, or volcanic rock. More ages of Anatolian summers and winters eroded this tuff into strange shapes—pyramids, cones, towers. Early Christians escaping from persecution came to Cappadocia, and found they were safe in caves hollowed out of the volcanic tuff. First they built rooms, high in the cones, accessible only by rope ladders. Then they began to cut churches and painted beautiful frescoes inside the cone walls. All this you can still see in Göreme valley, Ürgüp, Kılıçlar. Two famous cones have flat stones balanced on them like felt caps. Here is the Tokalı Kilise (Church of the Belt Buckle) with mosaics twelve centuries old, of the disciples fishing in the Sea of Galilee, and Elmalı Kilise (Church of the Apple), with images of saints painted on the ceilings.

No one knows exactly when or why the last hermit abandoned his cone hideout, but he left a rich legacy to the Turkish peasants who live here now. The cone rooms are cool in summer and warm in winter, and by scraping away the accumulated smoke put on the walls by the flueless chimneys, the modern inhabitants of Göreme are gradually enlarging their homes. The cool rooms are excellent places for weaving carpets, and a Cappadocian peasant girl in two years can turn out a carpet which will last several lifetimes, though she is certainly no competition for the machine age. The fields of this region have no true soil, only volcanic pumice, or powdered rock, which is excellent for growing fruits and vegetables. The rock houses not inhabited by people are full of pigeons, and these birds leave deposits of guano which the villagers collect to add to their income or use to fertilize their fields. As you can see, the thrifty Anatolian peasant has none of our feeling for the "fairy chimneys of Göreme"; he finds them useful in his daily life.

If you were to draw an equilateral triangle in Anatolia, with one angle based at Ankara and another at Kayseri, the third angle would have to land at Konya. This is the most Oriental-looking of Turkey's cities. It is an easy three-hour drive over an asphalt road from the capital, a road which did not exist in 1939. En route we pass through the "dead heart of Anatolia," and the huge salt lake called Tuz Gölü. It has no beaches, no boardwalk, no life at all except the villages of the salt workers. It has a very high salt concentration and the workers make their living cutting blocks of salt for sale in the bakkal and other places. We can see in the distance (the lake is several miles from the highway) the salt blocks piled in stiff white pyramids, like vanilla ice-cream cones.

Konya's physical setting is completely Oriental. Files of poplars intersect across its plain; green dots mark the outlines of pear orchards, and the city itself is a jumbled pile of mosques, minarets, and flat-roofed houses. It was once called Iconium, the city of icons, that is, images. The Christians who lived in Iconium were so pious that they carried images of Jesus, Mary, and the apostles, around with them. However, Konya is exclusively a Selcuk city. Most of its monuments date from the thirteenth century, when Sultan Alaeddin Kaikobad built the city into "New Rome."

Outside Konya are many well-preserved hans. The biggest, just north of the city, could easily have accommodated several camel caravans. Its walls are of rough fieldstone, fitted together without mortar, and very thick. In Selcuk times lookouts could watch the entire Konya plain from its high watchtowers. Over the arched entranceway are ancient signs in graceful Arabic lettering to tell the weary traveler he is safe and welcome. Shepherds use the hans for shelter from storms now, and a number of them are used by families to solve Turkey's housing problem.

Konya is a walled city, entered through a narrow gate. We twist down narrow dirt alleys, just wide enough for a car. Mud walls along the alleys connect the adobe houses, and the houses have no windows looking on the street. It is a queer feeling. Then suddenly we are on a wide boulevard, leading to a square, and parked in the square are horse-drawn carriages, shiny and black just like the ones in Central Park, New York.

This square is the center of the city; here is the *belediye* and its tourist bureau (a friendly Turk operating in a musty office heated by an old pot-bellied stove), the Turing Palas Oteli, best of a poor lot, and the shopping district. The square lies at the foot of an artificial hill. On the hill is a public park, and the solid buildings of Sultan Alaeddin's palace. Only the mosque is still in daily use, its stone floor covered with brilliant fringed prayer rugs. The *medrese* (Islamic religious school) was closed when education in Turkey became a public, not a church, affair; the palace is empty. All these brick structures are richly ornamented outside with fine writing, called calligraphy, and intricate lettered arabesques. The public park has nothing to do with the Selcuks, but in one of the flower beds is a little sign which somehow seems very appropriate for both the modern Turks, who love flowers, and the ancient Turks, with their Persian-inspired passion for artistic drawing. It reads: "Çiçeksiz bahçe, çocuksuz evi benzer" (A garden without flowers is like a house without children).

The finest Selcuk monument in Konya, and probably in all of Turkey, is the museum and *türbe* (tomb) of Mevlana. His real name was Jalal ad-Din Rumi, and he was born in Balkh, in what is now Afghanistan, where he taught philosophy and religion. Although he was a famous scholar-teacher in the Islamic world of the thirteenth century, he is remembered today primarily because he founded the order of Mevlevi, or Whirling Dervishes. The thirteenth century was a time of wars, Mongol invasions, and Crusades, but Konya was one of the few cities where philosophers could study in peace; so Rumi went to Konya. His patron there was the same Selcuk Sultan Alaeddin Kaikobad, an unusual ruler for the time because he encouraged art, poetry (which Rumi also wrote in quantity), and religious discussion. Hundreds of pious Moslems flocked to Konya to sit at Rumi's feet and study his mystical brand of Islam. When he died, he was buried on the grounds of the Mevlevi order, and his disciples erected a türbe of blue tile over his coffin—the one which we are now seeing.

Neither the leisurely carriage ride down Alaeddin Caddesi, nor the humble mud buildings around it, fully prepare us for Mevlana's tomb. The exterior colors are in perfect harmony, which suit the Mevlevi belief that harmony is the essence of religion. In the foreground, on a low wall, is a row of small pomegranate-shaped domes, each capped with a lead "helmet." Behind each dome is a small white minaret with a pointed lead cap. Two more tiers of larger lead domes lead our eyes upward to a single great dome, beside it a single tall minaret soaring upward, and to the right of the minaret is the fluted, dazzling blue spire of the türbe. In his life Mevlana taught that the way to know God was through dancing, and as he whirled in the Mevlevi dance he raised his arms as high as he could toward the sky, toward God. In the same way the minaret and türbe seem to be reaching toward heaven.

The interior of the tomb and museum are just as inspiring as the exterior, but in a different way. Here we are shown the cubicles where the dervishes studied and lived, and the great courtyard where they danced, their coarse wool robes spinning like skirts. Here also are great piles of carpets from all corners of Asia, brought as gifts to the Mevlevis, beautiful copies of the Koran in old Arabic, clocks, and many other art objects. The coffins of Mevlana and his relatives are covered with quilts embroidered in gold and silver thread. It doesn't seem at all odd to the Turks that they would worship Mevlana, founder of the reactionary Whirling Dervishes abolished by Ataturk. Mevlana is venerated not as a religious leader, but as an inspired poet. Each year the anniversary of his death, December 14, is observed in Konya with Mevlevi music and dancing.

The Oriental carpets which lie in such casual piles in the museum are not for sale, of course, but you can buy your own carpet in Konya. Just go to the factory and order it. Carpet weaving in Turkey today is done primarily by machine looms, in factories which have a sort of cooperative arrangement although they are owned separately. The Seli plant in Konya, for example, does some of the initial processes involved in making a Turkish carpet. Other processes take place at similar plants in nearby towns, Sille, Bor, and Karaman. Then the carpets are returned to Konya for drying, hanging, trimming, and sale. Isparta, another rug-making town, has its separate system and has given its name to a specific type of carpet. Although they can be ordered in all the traditional Oriental designs, Turkish carpets also come in solid colors, with a white fringe and a very deep pile; these have become so popular that in certain sizes they must be ordered three years in advance. In fact Turkish families have begun to invest money in carpets rather than real estate or stocks and bonds.

Konya is the gateway to the lake district, a dozen turquoise lakes in the middle of alpine scenery. Beyşehir, the largest, touches a snow-capped range at its southern end and a dam in flat marshy country at its northern extremity. The village of Beyşehir, which is anything but a resort, is at this end; otherwise all of the lake is deserted and no roads approach it. Fishermen moor their boats beside the dam; these are high-waisted, broad-beamed, made of rough planks, with a single stubby mast and gaff-rigged red sail. The old song "Red Sails in the Sunset" has real meaning when the Beyşehir fishing fleet comes home at dusk. The fishermen say that the lake is full of trout and landlocked salmon, and show with appropriate gestures the "one that got away." Not too many do, for fish is the staple of their diet. They have the lake to themselves. Not a house, not even a beachcomber's shack occupies the shoreline of magnificent sandy beaches.

Not too far away is the lake of Eğridir, a tiny lake which feeds into a much larger, marshy lake named Hayran Gölü. Otherwise Eğridir is encircled by snow-capped peaks. It might be labeled a mountain oasis, since the countryside around it is barren. The water is perpetually in motion, the winds roaring down the mountains to whip up froth on its shallow green waters. There is a Turkish army camp on the hills above Eğridir, and you will see many *askers* in their coarse wool O.D. uniforms strolling along the lake shore. The village of Eğridir itself, farther up the lake, has a Selcuk castle on an island, reached by a causeway. But it has no *otel*, not even a restaurant, nothing but a few dingy shops selling camel-saddles for the caravans which occasionally pass through. The nearest place where we can lay our heads is Isparta.

Isparta itself is a fascinating city, not because of its past, but because of its present industries. In addition to carpets, it has an attar of roses factory. Here rose petals are crushed to a dry powder, to form the base for most perfumes. You may expect a free sample, small-sized.

From Eğridir and Isparta a swing northward will bring us to another Anatolian sub-region, a region of rough mountains around the rim of the great central plain. Three smallish cities and one big one in this region rate more than a passing glance. The nearest is Akşehir, (The White City) a place of pilgrimage for all Turkophiles because it was the home of the almost-legendary national funnyman, Nasrettin Hoca. To go from Isparta and Eğridir direct to Akşehir is to contradict the saying that a short-cut is quicker than the long way around, and give the Hoca a good chuckle in his grave. For the nice red line on the map that seems to lead us straight to the city proves to be a treacherous shale-strewn road, winding over mountains, that drop sheer down for thousands of feet on both sides. The most terrifying experience I ever had in Turkey was here, inching my way through first a flock of sheep, then cows, and finally a camel caravan.

When finally reached, Akşehir is a clean, pretty little city. The Hoca's tomb is in a green garden at the foot of the mountain. It is round with a pointed lead cap, like the Döner Kumbet, but the arches are open, and round the base is an iron fence which has a center gate locked with a huge padlock. The fence ends in the back, however, and anyone can enter the tomb just by walking around. This is supposed to show Hoca's whimsical disregard of convention. The details of his life are somewhat contradictory, but he appears to have lived about the same time (fourteenth century) as Tamerlane, and unlike most people, to have pleased that builder of towers of skulls by his clever wit. He was first a schoolteacher (hoca means teacher) and traveled from place to place on a donkey to give his classes. His great reputation comes from his ability to deflate pompousness and satirize human weaknesses, and many of the practical, realistic attitudes of Turkish villagers are brought out clearly in Hoca stories. One of the most famous concerns the training of his donkey. Hoca decided to save money by cutting the donkey's food ration in half each day. He kept this up until the donkey got nothing to eat at all. One morning Hoca went to saddle the donkey and discovered that the animal was dead. He was very angry. "Just when I had trained my donkey to live on nothing," he cried, "it ups and dies on me!"

Afyon, another small city at the foot of the mountains, has many fields of scarlet poppies. The name Afyon means poppy, and poppies grow wild in many parts of Anatolia. But these Afyon poppies are special. They are cultivated for opium. The town has no opium dens though. These poppies are raised strictly for medicinal purposes.

Beyond Afyon, and easily accessible, are two cities which are, or could be, extremely important to Turkey's export trade. The first is Kütahya, a pottery town. Here is made the Kütahya ware mentioned earlier—thick earthen dishes, bowls, plates, and tiles decorated with birds, flowers, or traditional calligraphic designs in soft pastel colors, mostly greens, blues, and pale reds. Visitors are welcome at the potteries, where potters, who have learned their trade as apprentices from their fathers, turn these attractive dishes by hand on a wheel, using marvelous coordination of hand and eye instead of machine precision. The Kütahya ware makes handsome wall decoration; unfortunately it is extremely fragile and will crack when used for serving hot foods. Once the Turkish potters have solved these two problems, Kütahya ware will probably become a standard item in gift shops, as popular as Swedish or Danish china. Unlike these, it has a genuine handmade, hand-painted look about it.

The second city is Eskişehir, important because it is the center of the meerschaum industry. Turkey is one of the world's largest producers of this soft white stone used for making smoking pipes. If you wish you can choose your own block of meerschaum from any shop in Eskişehir and have a pipe made from it, to any size and specification. One man I know had his profile carved on a meerschaum, although for some odd reason the plain block pipes smoke much better than the fancy carved ones do.

Turkey's southern region offers perhaps the greatest tourist potential. A great part of it is roadless; many ruined palaces in the Taurus and along the coast have been swallowed up in the underbrush. The two ends of this Turkish Riviera are quite accessible. The Riviera goes from Antalya eastward, curving around the Mediterranean coastline. From Ankara, we reach the eastern portion by penetrating the Cilician Gates, traditional route of northern conquerors invading the warm lands to the south, Syria, Lebanon, Palestine. In the 1830's the Egyptian general Ibrahim Pasha, son of the ruler of Egypt at that time, Mohammed Ali, reversed the process. He blasted a road through solid rock for his cannon and horse-drawn wagons, in order to lead his army through the Taurus range to attack the Sultan. Now both a railroad and a highway, within a few feet of each other in places, creep through the pass; we can thank Ibrahim for this improved transportation. Having left the Gates, we are literally outside Anatolia, in the wide alluvial plain of Adana. Here are Turkey's cotton-growing center, Tarsus, which has nothing to remind us of its most famous citizen, St. Paul, and around the corner of the Mediterranean, the Turkish province called the Hatay, which includes Antioch. This city, now Antakya, is the place where Jesus' followers were first called Christians, and where

St. Peter preached, in a little stone church still standing in a willow grove.

The eastern part of the Riviera proper, from the port of Mersin to Silifke where the road ends abruptly in a sand dune, is rather depressing. When Rome was powerful five million people lived on this coast. Pompey the Great, Caesar's rival, built a city here that was supposed to make his name immortal. Acres of ruin mark it now, nothing exists except a few sheep grazing in the market place. What happened to all this life? One raid too many, military conquest, floods—or some minor thing like the drying up of the water supply? Whatever the reason, Pompeipopolis and its sister cities are among the saddest, loneliest places on earth—but not so lonely as Anamur, the town on the tip of the "buffalo's whiskers," at the bottom of Asia Minor. There is just enough life in Anamur to make it unutterably lonely; the handful of villagers have no trade, little to do except stare at their majestic Selcuk castle on the bay. They are outnumbered, in fact surrounded, by the dead—by a great city of tombs and temples, Anemorium, "the city of anemones." One day the coast road will reach Anamur, and *then* the villagers will pick the anemones that grow in the crevices, and offer them in bunches to visitors, as they must have done a thousand years ago.

There are no Cilician Gates through the Taurus at the western end of the Riviera. There are a few narrow passes, and the road follows the courses of little alpine valleys, surprisingly warm and free from snow even in the dead of winter. The mountaineers build their homes of sandstone or limestone, half-timbered, and raise a pretty good crop of barley. The mountains are heavily wooded, with forests of pine, cedar, juniper, and the valonia oak, an important source of wealth, as its acorns, dried, are used in tanning leather. Scattered through the woods are colonies of *tahtacis*, woodcutters. They belong to a different religious sect from the rest of the Turks, although they are still Moslems. Long ago they were given the right to cut wood in the Taurus, exclusively, to mark them as different from the main body of the Turks, and they still keep the job.

In the Taurus, too, are the Yürüks, wandering nomads whose origin is as obscure as that of gypsies. They speak a special dialect of Turkish, very hard to understand. Their countrymen call them the original Turks because their blood is pure, not intermixed. They are Moslems, believing in Allah, but they are very superstitious and believe that spirits inhabit rocks, trees, and the sky. They keep the old costumes; the women wear necklaces of coins, which make them walking safe-deposit boxes. The lives of the Yürüks follow a never-changing pattern—seven months in the lowlands, five months in the hills. The trek of a Yürük clan from summer to winter camp, and vice versa, is a complicated affair; everything must be mobile. Each camel carries two huge saddlebags packed with pillows, bedding, tents etc., the donkeys each carry smaller saddlebags, and usually a child perched atop the load. The Yürük women lead the animals; the men ride or walk ahead, scouting the trails. Long lines of black goats and sheep, and young camels, follow the procession. In camp the women unpack, unroll the long strips of colored felt used to make the tents, scour the big brass cooking-pots until they shine, cook, look after innumerable children. Then the men take over. They build the cooking-fires, and settle back in groups to smoke their rolled cigarettes and talk. What a division of labor!

At the top of the Taurus watershed, on Güllük Dağ (Rose Mountain), is the ruined city of Termessos. Its theater, market, and temples are literally hidden in spring under flowers—roses, pansies, daisies, and sweet-smelling bay and myrtle. Far below, the mountain falls away to a sparkling white line. The local villager who acts as guide to Termessos points down. "Deniz, akdeniz" (The sea, the white sea), he says reverently. In his voice is the age-old longing of the mountain man for the sea, and the unknown lands beyond.

Below the Taurus is the little seaport of Antalya, headquarters for the western end of the Riviera. The setting is ideal for a resort town.

A string of pink and white houses with corrugated tile roofs curves around a doll-sized harbor full of lowslung Mediterranean caiques. Across the harbor to the west are the rugged slopes of Mt. Climax and Mt. Solyma; the legend says that roses bloom on the latter's snowy summit. These mountains drop almost straight down to the beach. Behind Antalya the Taurus rises into the sky, blue against a deeper blue. No wonder it is Turkey's picture-postcard town!

Antalya has its drawbacks. Accommodations are painfully plain at the two adequate hotels, the Yayla Palas and Turistik Palas. There is no night life, nothing to buy, not a decent restaurant even by Anatolian standards. Antalyans have not yet realized that a tourist is a being different from themselves. Let us hope they don't, for with a little effort anyone can make his own amusement there. Carriages like those in Konya—perhaps the same ones, transmitted on some magic carpet —are available; Antalya can be pretty hot during the day, but when the first evening breeze steals in from the sea, the horses' ears prick up and they begin to shuffle their feet. The clip-clop of their hoofs on the cobblestones matches the soft rushing of water, hidden from view. For Antalya is a town built on water. The icy Taurus streams that irrigate the Riviera plain rush down the mountainsides and would continue straight into the sea, but the people of Antalya have built stone conduits in the islands of the town's two main boulevards, and thus channeled this water so that it flows placidly downhill to the public park. Those streams not managed in this way are left alone; most of them flow underground, under the town, and wherever they come up above ground they are channeled under little wooden footbridges. Antalya is proud of its water. One of the last sounds we hear from our hotel balcony at night is the street sweeper laying the dust, dipping and filling big petrol tins from a stream by the side of the road.

Antalya and its hinterland are subtropical, due to the sea and the mountain wall protecting them from winter winds. Almost every kind of flower and tree grows there. Palm trees line the main boulevards, and houses are half-hidden behind wisteria vines, brilliant oleander and bougainvillea. Banana palms grow on street corners, and oranges and lemons in large plantations just outside of town.

This Riviera capital is at its colorful best during Şeker Bayram. This festival, officially three days but known to disrupt business for a week, comes immediately after the end of Ramazan, the month of fasting which Moslems observe. During Ramazan they may neither eat nor drink from the moment of sunrise, until that moment after sunset when a black thread cannot be distinguished from a white one. Life slows to a crawl everywhere in Turkey during this month, but when black and white look the same on the last day, a cannon booms, and a spirit half-relief and half-anticipation sweeps over the country. People begin to fill the streets, dressed in their best clothes. Many wear old Ottoman costumes, saved for such occasions. Children wear new clothes, for Şeker Bayram corresponds to Christmas in being expensive for Father. Each child carries a handkerchief knotted with a coin in one corner. Families pay visits to their relatives, beginning with the older ones, and exchange gifts of candy, since Şeker Bayram means The Festival of Sugar. The children, of course, really gorge themselves; the candy stores of Antalya are jammed with parents solemnly watching their offspring trying to decide which sweets they will have.

The vividness of the costumes is complemented by the pushcarts of the concessionaires. The *limonata* man pushes a cart painted yellow and hung with paper streamers; the *gazoz* man (he sells Turkish ginger ale) has a green cart; the perfume lady, with a blue cart, sprays each customer with a shot of attar of rose water. The most popular salesman is the iceman, who sells ice (unboiled) by the cube. Behind the hotel a vintage Ferris wheel begins to creak upward with its load of shrieking children. The holiday is on in earnest—for three days no business will be done in Antalya.

The old section of Antalya is walled, and the new part has grown up outside these walls. The entrance is through an opening called Hadrian's Gate. The streets of the old town are narrow cobbled lanes, and the houses have overhanging wooden balconies and latticed windows, like old English villages. You can hire a rowboat or caique on the wharf, and ride up the coast, under the slitted windows of a tower called the Hīdīrlīk, that once served archers defending the town from pirates. The Mediterranean is deep blue, perfectly clear. The cliffs on both sides of Antalya's harbor drop sheer into the sea, and every few hundred yards waterfalls, called Catarrhactes, send up great clouds of spray as the fresh water hits the salt. These waterfalls are really the runoff from the many streams that rise in the Taurus; fed with snow, they race downhill without stopping until they reach the sea. One of the larger ones is called Düden; it falls over a concealed cave, where a princess once hid to escape from slave traders. She was never found, but the cave echoes with a hollow moaning sound which may or may not be hers.

Antalya also has a large handsome park, called Inönü Park, on the seawall above the Hīdīrlīk. It was built by a vali (governor) who had been to Vienna and so admired the famous Prater there that he decided to duplicate it in his home town. The park with its magnificent palm trees, oleanders, flowers watered diligently twice a day by old women is essential to Antalya's colorful postcard look.

The rest of the Turkish Riviera stretches eastward from Antalya along a wide, almost harborless bay. Here, too, are the ruins of great cities, like Perge. A great Roman aqueduct still brings water to Perge, or would if anyone were left to drink it. Nearby is Aspendos, with the finest Roman theater in Turkey so well preserved that we can see Shakespeare performed (in Turkish) there in October.

We stop for a picnic lunch near Aspendos, under ancient willows, and watch the placid flow of the Köprü Irmak (River of the Bridge), so named because a magnificent stone Selcuk bridge of seven arches crosses it. It is impossible to believe that Aspendos was a seaport twenty centuries ago, but a lot of silt has gone up the river since then. At the door to the theater, past and present meet as they so often do in Turkey. Two young merchants offer us, not first-row tickets at inflated prices, but Greek and Roman coins picked up in the furrows.

Unfortunately they are not as valuable, or rare, as these sellers would have us think.

Aspendos's neighbor is Side, once a haunt of pirates and slave traders. We have a glass of *ayran* by the sea, under a pergola roofed with grape-vines, on the most beautiful beach in Turkey, a long white crescent. No wonder Mark Antony and Cleopatra spent their last romantic hours here! Neither bathers nor honeymooners come to Side now; the beach is used primarily as a road by peasants leading their donkeys to market. What they think of Cleopatra has not been recorded, but they become quite annoyed by having to detour around our sand-covered bodies.

This Riviera road ends for all practical purposes some seventy miles further, at Alanya, the other "living" town on the coast. Alanya is extremely popular with people who suffer from asthma and other re-spiratory diseases. They come from hundreds of miles to take the cure in its damp salt-air caves. But it, too, is a romantic place in the old tradition, with its superb Red Tower (Kizil Kule), its seven-hundred-year-old Selcuk shipyard which turns out fishing boats without modern machinery, and its graceful citadel. We turn back from Alanya with regret.

10. Home to Istanbul

WHAT TURKEY is probably going to look like, fifteen or twenty years from now, depends on conditions outside the country. "Give us twenty years of peace," the Turks say, "and you will see what we can do." They ask only peace, real peace, which would allow them to reduce the size of their standing army of sixteen divisions, and divert over half their national income from military expenditures into peacetime development. Modern Turkey wants, and needs, many things, things which we take for granted—things like hospitals, factories, millions of automobiles, superhighways, supermarkets, a life of leisure aided by mechanical gadgets.

There are some qualities peculiar to the Turks, but one quality which they share with Americans, Englishmen, Arabs, in fact all peoples of the earth, is their desire to be left alone. They are realists, and they know that international understanding is the key to progress. They also know that the main threat to their security, their happiness, comes from one direction—a cold wind from north of the Black Sea.

Until they can let their guard down, certain that military power is as outdated as the witch doctor, the Turks are going ahead with what tools they can afford. These tools are used pretty effectively; we will see examples everywhere. The Sakarya River, where the nationalist armies stopped the Greek invasion back in 1921, no longer flows wastefully along its erratic course; the huge Sarīyar Dam extracts hydroelectric power to turn on Ankara's lights. At Tuzla the General Motors assembly plant is beginning to turn out jeeps by the thousand for Turkey's farmers; these also carry schoolteachers and agricultural experts into the isolated regions. Every month Turkey moves a little farther toward catching the Western nations she has chosen to emulate.

This determined progressiveness unites all the Turks, whatever their individual feelings about the best way to do it. The election campaign of 1957 was bitterly fought. Former President Inönü's People's Republican Party (the party founded by Ataturk) attacked the Democrat Government for trying to do everything at once, causing ruinous inflation and shortages in every commodity from coffee to bathtub stoppers. Turkish newspapers, not noted for their high ethical standards, began to print critical editorials of government policy. The Grand National Assembly passed strict laws to control the press and stop the opposition from election campaigning. It was a surprise, therefore, that the elections were held two months ahead of schedule. In effect the Government said to the Turkish people, "We believe our way is better than Mr. Inönü's for making Turkey strong, and we are asking you to support us now, not wait until spring when things may be better."

The election results were overwhelmingly in favor of the Democrats. President Celal Bayar was returned to office, and Prime Minister Adnan Menderes given a free hand for his program. There is a word in the Islamic religion, *tariqah,* which means literally way. It refers to the path that each Moslem follows toward understanding God and making full use of his abilities. The Turkish nation chose its tariqah under Ataturk; in 1950 it voted to change the leadership but not the way; in 1954 and 1957 it reaffirmed this way toward full use of its abilities, in religion and politics alike.

We have traveled a circular route through Anatolia in order to find our own way "home to Istanbul." This route serves as a sort of training ground for Turkey's queen city. Looking back on the journey, we find that every experience has somehow helped to prepare us for the return. There was the heady excitement of Ankara, an aggressively modern metropolis squarely in the middle of the lonely plateau. After a long day's drive through this plateau, through dust, and silent villages, the lights of Ankara are a welcome sight for the stranger. The welcome received in some of Anatolia's villages has helped ease this loneliness; we understand better the Turkish character and its essential worth, from the hospitality of the village coffeehouses.

Ancient history, so deeply imbedded in the Turkish soil, has come alive for us in the great ruined cities of the south. We have shared in the experiences of the anchorites who carved and painted their Christian beliefs in the cones of Ürgüp and Göreme. We have been properly inspired by Mevlana's blue-tile tomb. As travelers seeking new worlds, we have picked poppies on Taurus mountain meadows, we have splashed in the turquoise water of secret lakes, climbed the roofs of Selcuk hans like defenders of old, to signal with flashlights across the mountains the threat of an attack. We have dreamed on the sand of Side, under the Levantine sun, while peasants pick their way carefully around our feet.

More recently, we have gone to Izmir, Turkey's third city and headquarters of the North Atlantic Treaty Organization (NATO); Turkey is a full member. Because of its harbor and its importance as the outlet of a rich agricultural region, Izmir's resurrection after the 1922 fire was inevitable. Turkey's most important exports, figs, sultanas, raisins, chrome ore, are carried out to deep water on lighters, loaded onto freighters, and eventually reach our factories and dinner tables from Izmir. At the International Fair held annually in Izmir's Kulturpark, August 20—September 20, American TV and refrigerators compete with Soviet machinery.

I mentioned earlier the special air, clear and stimulating, of Anatolia. Izmir has its special air, the "violet air" of ancient Ionia. Remember the "wine-dark" Aegean Sea in Homer's *Iliad?* Homer wrote about "violet Ionia" in the same epic; although we do not know where the blind poet was born, it may have been Smyrna, the old name of Izmir. From the top of the city's dominant landmark, Kadifekale (velvet castle), we were far removed from the busy activity of the harbor, and could almost see the velvet. If Homer was not born there, he was surely inspired by Kadifekale.

Izmir also reminds us of Ephesus, where three great cultures, three civilizations, sleep in marble harmony. Representing Christianity are the Cave of the Seven Sleepers, seven young men who slept longer than Rip Van Winkle and woke up to find that their religion had become respectable; the Panaya Kapulu, perhaps the last home on earth of the Virgin Mary, and the church of St. John. The Greeks and Romans left a great stadium, an avenue paved entirely of marble blocks, temples and libraries. The Turks added minarets, to make the Christian churches into mosques, or built their own mosques. They have the last word since the modern town of Ephesus is called Selcuk. But this combination of civilizations gives Ephesus a universal appeal; like Jerusalem, it belongs to the world.

The way back to Istanbul also leads through Bursa, twenty-five hundred years old, yet the most Turkish of all Anatolia's cities. Bursa proves once and for all that the old Turks were a civilized, artistic people. The early sultans, in fact the first five, made their capital in Bursa, leaving behind them magnificent mosques and tombs to remember them by. The mosques of Bursa proved to be a challenge to our feet second only to those of Istanbul; mosque-trotting is hard on the socks, because shoes must be removed before entering a mosque. However, the beautiful deep green tiles of the Green Mosque (Yeşil Cami) of Mehmet I, Murad II's mosque, a mosaic of blue Persian tiles, and many others, are worth the trotting.

Quite interesting, also, are the tombs, simple octagonal buildings of plain tiles in gardens of roses and cypress trees, reflecting the simplicity of their occupants who created a mighty empire but asked little for themselves. Bursa is profoundly impressive in other ways, too. One of its little habits, as we found out when we took a drive, is not to cut down a tree. The streets thus go around the trees, and it is impossible to get anywhere in a hurry. Bursans hurry only when on the ski slopes of Uludağ (Mount Olympus of Mysia, not to be confused with Mt.

Olympus in Greece). This broad mountain gives "the fortunate city" its ski slopes and its never-failing water supply, its natural hot springs, which are piped into the water systems of the hotels to give guests a room with private Turkish bath.

So we return to Istanbul, itself just a stage-stop on a much longer journey back to our real home, keenly alive to Turkey's possibilities and aware of Turkish behavior. Still Istanbul will do as a temporary home, at least if the bulldozer leaves enough of it. In the short time we were away more of the city has been leveled. The waterfront along the Golden Horn and Galata, particularly, are naked without their covering of small crowded houses and wooden apartment buildings. As we move around, however, the purpose of Prime Minister Menderes— "Adnan the builder," he is now called—is plain. Nothing has really changed in Istanbul except the means of getting around.

This city which has known so much bloodshed and conflict is a nervous city. We find none of the placidity of the Anatolians in Istanbul. Anatolian people who come to live here soon become as nervous as the old residents. The nervousness of Istanbul is highly charged with energy, however; for the first time we can understand why the Ankarians rush down here in summer like lemmings to the sea. Down on the waterfront are some nervous types. "Balik, taze balik!" (Fish, fresh fish), cry the fish peddlers, and they dangle their varied catch, red mullet, tunny, mackerel, in front of us, determined to make a sale. On the lower level of the Galata Bridge we find the *balik kebabçis;* instead of lamb, they fry fish steaks in a pan. Served hot inside a loaf of bread, for about a lira, they make us forget the şiş kebab of Anatolia very quickly. Equally nervous are the men who sell *simits,* a kind of crescent-shaped pretzel, from trays which they balance on top of their heads. Every now and again some fall off into the dust, but this does not seem to affect their taste, and so long as we are not looking they are quickly replaced on the tray.

Much of Istanbul, of course, is connected with the past. Although it has a million people, the city is more or less separated into municipalities which straggle along the low hills paralleling the Bosphorus, both on the European and the Asiatic sides. We find that the rebuilding program allows us to find these monuments much more easily than we had expected to from the guidebook. The palaces are easy enough because of their distinctive construction; Dolma Bahçe, like Versailles on the water, the Seraglio (Turkish Topkapī Saray), Beylerbey where King Edward VIII stayed and encouraged Ataturk to revive traditional Turkish music (perhaps the least constructive reform of the Republic). The great mosques and Byzantine churches (Istanbul has 444 mosques) are also easy for us to find, although this is not true of many of the Byzantine relics. The Turks, being Moslems, accept Christianity as a fellow-religion, and in this century they have encouraged the restoration of the magnificent Byzantine mosaics inside these churches. We can watch Byzantinologists, including fellow-Americans, at work with toothbrush and rag, bringing to light the mosaics of the Kariye Cami, hidden for centuries under many coats of plaster. The work at St. Sophia, Istanbul's most famous building, is complete; this structure was first called the Great Church, named Hagia Sophia which means divine wisdom. It has been burned, rebuilt, burned again, rebuilt, used for five centuries as a mosque, and by order of Ataturk has been turned into a museum; now its troubles are over except for tourists.

The skyline of Istanbul is Turkish, not Byzantine. Without its spires and domes, the city would be an ugly one. The Blue Mosque of Sultan Ahmed, across the street from St. Sophia, is the only one in the world with six minarets. The builder, in his haste to complete it, forgot that this honor was reserved for the Great Mosque in Mecca, where good Moslems go on their pilgrimages. Since it was too late to change Ahmed's mosque, the Great Mosque was given a seventh minaret, and everybody was satisfied.

We couldn't possibly visit all of Istanbul's mosques, and would not really want to, as they are alike except for decoration and size. One of the mosques, however, contains more of the spirit of Istanbul than the others. It is the mosque of Eyüp, the standard-bearer of Mohammed. Eyüp is venerated as a saint; his bones were conveniently discovered during the siege of 1453. Now they rest in a simple tomb behind an equally simple white marble mosque, which contains the sword of the Prophet. Because of this double holiness, we find pious Turks praying there, fingering their *tesbih* (a sort of rosary) of thirty-three or ninety-nine beads. Other Turks feed the doves in the courtyard; octogenarians smoke water-pipes under the plane trees. The cemeteries around Eyüp have their headstones tipped at crazy angles, a Turkish burial custom that developed because of the belief that death must be full of ups and downs, since life is.

Higher on the hill is the little café where Pierre Loti, a French novelist, wrote several of his fantasies, inspired, no doubt, by the scene before him. It is the most romantic place in a romantic city. The view inspires everyone who comes there to dream—the minarets and domes of Old Istanbul, the ships and caiques in the Bosphorus, the crescent-shaped Golden Horn, and the little brook oddly named the Sweet Waters of Europe (there is one in Asia, too), where Ottoman princesses used to come on picnics and sometimes meet their lovers.

It is difficult to leave Istanbul. Every day spent there brings a keener sense of frustration; there is so much to see, to sense, to do. We have been to the Great Bazaar, that combination of craft guilds and flea market which is peculiar to Istanbul; while we didn't find a rarity such as Empress Josephine's bracelet, we did manage to collect a fair amount of Turkish "loot" for gifts, as Istanbul is almost the only city in Turkey with a wide selection. We brought the title of Yeats' poem, "Sailing to Byzantium" to life when we rode a ferryboat all the way up the Bosphorus to the Black Sea and back. Anatolia, Turkey's massive heartland, seems almost unreal when you are busy in Istanbul. But don't be fooled. The same sturdy spirit animates both parts of Turkey; the same characteristics exist in city and plain.

There is no guarantee that you will come back to Turkey. The practical Turks have no charming superstition that says you will, simply by tossing a coin into a fountain. But their leave-taking holds in it the seeds of hope. "Allahaismarladik" (good-bye), you say to them, and they reply "Güle, güle gidiniz!" (Go happily). No one could do otherwise.

Index